Keto Diet

Cookbook for Beginners 2023

1800 Days of Delicious and Nourishing Keto Recipes to Achieve Your Weight Loss Goals and Improve Your Health Incl. 28-Day Meal Plan

Poppy Charlton

CONTENTS

Introduction

Are you ready to embark on a tantalizing journey towards achieving your weight loss goals and improving your overall health? Look no further than the Keto Diet Cookbook for Beginners 2023, a comprehensive guide to the ketogenic lifestyle crafted by yours truly, Poppy Charlton, a certified nutritionist and passionate advocate for healthy living.

As someone who has personally experienced the transformative power of the keto diet, I felt compelled to share my knowledge and expertise with beginners looking to embrace this lifestyle. This cookbook is the culmination of years of research, experimentation, and a deep commitment to empowering individuals to take control of their health and well-being.

What sets this cookbook apart is its collection of 1800 days of delicious and nourishing keto recipes. Gone are the days of bland and repetitive meals on a diet. I believe that taste and variety are key to sustainable and enjoyable eating habits. That's why I have curated a diverse range of recipes that not only satisfy your cravings but also align with the principles of the ketogenic diet. From mouthwatering breakfast options to satisfying lunches, indulgent dinners, and even guilt-free desserts, this cookbook offers a wide array of flavors and textures to keep you excited about your keto journey.

But this cookbook goes beyond just recipes. It includes a comprehensive 28-day meal plan that takes the guesswork out of your keto experience. No more struggling to figure out what to eat or how to balance your macronutrients.

By following the Keto Diet Cookbook for Beginners 2023, you can expect to experience a multitude of benefits. Not only will you shed excess weight and achieve your desired physique, but you'll also notice increased energy levels, improved mental clarity, stabilized blood sugar levels, and enhanced overall well-being. This book equips you with the tools, knowledge, and support needed to make the keto lifestyle a sustainable and enjoyable part of your everyday life.

Get ready to embark on a tantalizing journey towards a healthier and more vibrant you with this cookbook as your trusted companion. Let the flavors and benefits of the keto diet transform your life, one delicious recipe at a time. Embrace the power of the keto lifestyle and unlock a world of culinary possibilities that will nourish your body and delight your taste buds.

What is the Keto Diet exactly?

The Keto Diet, short for ketogenic diet, is a low-carbohydrate, high-fat diet that has gained popularity for its potential health benefits and weight loss effects. The main principle behind the Keto Diet is to drastically reduce the intake of carbohydrates and replace them with healthy fats. By doing so, the body enters a metabolic state called ketosis, where it becomes highly efficient at burning fat for energy instead of relying on glucose from carbohydrates.

In a typical Keto Diet, the macronutrient breakdown is approximately 70-75% of calories from fat, 20-25% from protein, and only 5-10% from carbohydrates. This significant reduction in carbohydrates forces the body to shift its primary fuel source from glucose to ketones, which are produced when fat is broken down.

The Keto Diet emphasizes whole, unprocessed foods such as meat, fish, eggs, dairy, nuts, seeds, healthy oils, and non-starchy vegetables. It restricts or eliminates foods high in carbohydrates, including grains, legumes, sugars, and most fruits.

The benefits of the Keto Diet may include weight loss, increased satiety, improved mental clarity and focus, stabilized blood sugar levels, reduced inflammation, and improved overall metabolic health. However, it's important to note that the Keto Diet may not be suitable for everyone and should be approached with caution, especially for those with certain medical conditions or on specific medications.

What are the benefits of using a Keto Diet?

The Keto Diet has gained popularity due to its potential benefits for various aspects of health and well-being. While individual results may vary, here are some potential benefits associated with following a Keto Diet:

- **Weight loss**

One of the primary reasons people adopt the Keto Diet is for weight loss. The low-carbohydrate, high-fat nature of the diet can lead to a reduction in overall calorie intake and an increase in the body's fat-burning capabilities. When carbohydrates are restricted, the body turns to stored fat as its primary fuel source, resulting in weight loss.

- **Increased satiety**

The high-fat content of the Keto Diet can help promote feelings of fullness and reduce cravings. Fat takes longer to digest, which can help control appetite and prevent overeating. This increased satiety can be beneficial for those trying to manage their calorie intake and maintain a healthy weight.

- **Improved blood sugar control**

The Keto Diet has shown promise in helping manage blood sugar levels, particularly for individuals with type 2 diabetes or insulin resistance. By limiting carbohydrate intake, the body produces less glucose, which can help stabilize blood sugar levels and reduce insulin spikes.

- **Enhanced mental clarity and focus**

Some individuals report improved cognitive function and mental clarity while following a Keto Diet. The brain can efficiently utilize ketones as an alternative energy source, providing a steady supply of fuel and potentially reducing brain fog or mental fatigue.

- **Increased energy levels**

When the body transitions into a state of ketosis, it becomes efficient at burning fat for fuel. This can lead to more sustained energy levels throughout the day, as fat provides a longer-lasting and more stable source of energy compared to carbohydrates.

- **Reduced inflammation**

The Keto Diet may have anti-inflammatory effects due to its focus on whole, unprocessed foods and the reduction of inflammatory foods such as sugar and refined carbohydrates. Chronic inflammation is associated with various health conditions, and by reducing inflammation, the Keto Diet may help improve overall health and well-being.

- **Improved lipid profile**

Contrary to what one might expect from a high-fat diet, the Keto Diet has been shown to improve lipid profiles in some individuals. It can increase levels of HDL (good) cholesterol, lower levels of LDL (bad) cholesterol, and reduce triglyceride levels, all of which are important markers for cardiovascular health.

What are some common ingredients in a Keto Diet?

The Keto Diet focuses on consuming foods that are low in carbohydrates and high in healthy fats. Here are some common ingredients in a Keto Diet:

- **Healthy fats**

Healthy fats are a staple in the Keto Diet. Some common sources of healthy fats include avocados, coconut oil, olive oil, butter, ghee, and fatty cuts of meat like salmon or beef.

- **Low-carbohydrate vegetables**

Non-starchy vegetables are an important part of the Keto Diet as they provide essential vitamins, minerals, and fiber. Some examples are leafy greens (spinach, kale, arugula), broccoli, cauliflower, zucchini, bell peppers, and asparagus.

- **Protein sources**

Protein is essential for muscle repair and growth. Good sources of protein in the Keto Diet include meat (beef, chicken, pork, lamb), fish (salmon, tuna, sardines), eggs, and tofu.

- **Full-fat dairy**

Full-fat dairy products can be included in the Keto Diet. Examples include cheese, yogurt, and heavy cream. However, it is important to watch for added sugars in flavored or sweetened dairy products.

- **Nuts and seeds**

Nuts and seeds are a great source of healthy fats and fiber. Some keto-friendly options include almonds, walnuts, macadamia nuts, flaxseeds, chia seeds, and pumpkin seeds. However, portion control is important as they can be calorie-dense.

- **Low-carb fruits**

While fruits are generally limited on the Keto Diet due to their natural sugar content, some fruits can be consumed in moderation. Examples include berries (strawberries, blueberries, raspberries), which are lower in carbohydrates compared to other fruits.

- **Herbs and spices**

Herbs and spices are used to enhance flavor without adding extra carbohydrates. Examples include garlic, ginger, turmeric, basil, oregano, rosemary, and cumin.

- **Low-carb sweeteners**

Some individuals on the Keto Diet may choose to use low-carb sweeteners to satisfy their sweet cravings. Examples include stevia, erythritol, monk fruit extract, and xylitol. However, moderation is key as some people may experience digestive issues with certain sweeteners.

- **Alternative flours**

Traditional wheat flour is high in carbohydrates, so the Keto Diet often uses alternative flours. These include almond flour, coconut flour, flaxseed meal, and psyllium husk powder to make keto-friendly baked goods and bread substitutes.

- **Condiments and sauces**

Many condiments and sauces can be high in added sugars and carbohydrates. On the Keto Diet, it's important to read labels and choose options that are low in carbohydrates. Examples include mustard, mayonnaise, hot sauce, soy sauce (check for low-sugar versions), and sugar-free salad dressings.

It's worth noting that the specific foods and ingredients in a Keto Diet may vary based on individual preferences, dietary restrictions, and cultural backgrounds. It is always important to listen to your body, choose high-quality ingredients, and ensure you are meeting your nutritional needs while following the Keto Diet.

Can I still enjoy desserts or snacks while following a Keto Diet?

Yes, you can still enjoy desserts and snacks while following a Keto Diet, although they will need to be modified to fit within the low-carbohydrate guidelines. Here are some ideas for keto-friendly desserts and snacks:

- **Dark chocolate**

Choose dark chocolate with a high percentage of cocoa (70% or higher) and limited added sugars. Enjoy a small piece as an occasional treat.

- **Berries with whipped cream**

Berries like strawberries, blueberries, and raspberries are relatively low in carbohydrates. Enjoy a serving of berries with a dollop of unsweetened whipped cream for a sweet treat.

- **Keto fat bombs**

Fat bombs are high-fat, low-carb treats that can satisfy your cravings. They are typically made with ingredients like coconut oil, nut butter, cocoa powder, and low-carb sweeteners. There are many recipes available online for different flavors, such as chocolate, peanut butter, or coconut.

- **Cheese and nuts**

Pairing cheese with nuts, such as almonds or macadamia nuts, can create a satisfying and keto-friendly snack. Just be mindful of portion sizes as nuts can be calorie-dense.

- **Greek yogurt with low-carb toppings**

Greek yogurt is relatively low in carbohydrates and high in protein. Opt for full-fat, unsweetened Greek yogurt and add toppings such as crushed nuts, chia seeds, or a sprinkle of cinnamon for added flavor.

- **Avocado pudding**

Avocado can be used to make a creamy and delicious pudding. Blend ripe avocados with cocoa powder, a low-carb sweetener, and a splash of almond milk for a keto-friendly dessert.

- **Keto-friendly cookies and bars**

There are many recipes available for keto-friendly cookies and bars made with alternative flours, such as almond or coconut flour, and sweetened with low-carb sweeteners. These can be a good option for a sweet treat while following a Keto Diet.

- **Pork rinds or kale chips**

For a crunchy snack, try pork rinds (which are carb-free) or homemade kale chips that are baked with olive oil and seasonings.

- **Keto smoothies**

You can make delicious and satisfying smoothies using low-carb fruits like berries, low-carb vegetables, a source of healthy fats (such as avocado or coconut milk), and a low-carb protein powder or nut butter.

- **Homemade beef jerky**

Make your own beef jerky by marinating lean beef in a low-carb marinade and dehydrating it. This can be a convenient and protein-rich snack.

It's important to note that while these options can be enjoyed in moderation, portion control is still essential to ensure you stay within your recommended calorie and carbohydrate limits. Additionally, always check the ingredients and nutritional information of packaged snacks or desserts to ensure they fit within the Keto Diet guidelines.

Appetizers, Snacks & Side Dishes Recipes

Middle Eastern Style Tuna Salad

Servings: 6

Cooking Time: 0 Minutes

Ingredients:

- ¼ cup chopped pitted ripe olives
- ¼ cup drained and chopped roasted red peppers
- 2 green onions, sliced
- 2 pcs of 6-oz cans of tuna in water, drained and flaked
- 6 cups salad greens like lettuce
- ¼ cup Mayonnaise

Directions:

1. Except for salad greens, mix all the ingredients in a bowl.
2. Arrange salad greens on the bottom of the bowl and top with tuna mixture.
3. Serve and enjoy.

Nutrition Info:

- Info Per Servings 3g Carbs, 3g Protein, 8g Fat, 92 Calories

Zucchini Gratin With Feta Cheese

Servings: 6

Cooking Time: 65 Minutes

Ingredients:

- Cooking spray
- 2 lb zucchinis, sliced
- 2 red bell peppers, seeded and sliced
- Salt and black pepper to taste
- 1 ½ cups crumbled feta cheese
- ⅓ cup crumbled feta cheese for topping
- 2 tbsp butter
- ¼ tsp xanthan gum
- ½ cup heavy whipping cream

Directions:

1. Preheat oven to 370ºF. Place the sliced zucchinis in a colander over the sink, sprinkle with salt and let sit for 20 minutes. Transfer to paper towels to drain the excess liquid.
2. Grease a baking dish with cooking spray and make a layer of zucchini and bell peppers in the dish overlapping one on another. Season with black pepper, and sprinkle with some feta cheese. Repeat the layering process a second time.
3. Combine the butter, xanthan gum, and whipping cream in a microwave dish for 2 minutes, stir to mix completely, and pour over the vegetables. Top with remaining feta cheese.
4. Bake the gratin for 45 minutes to be golden brown on top. Cut out slices and serve with kale salad.

Nutrition Info:

- Info Per Servings 4g Carbs, 14g Protein, 21g Fat, 264 Calories

Crunchy Pork Rind And Zucchini Sticks

Servings: 4
Cooking Time: 20 Minutes
Ingredients:
- Cooking spray
- ¼ cup pork rind crumbs
- 1 tsp sweet paprika
- ¼ cup shredded Parmesan cheese
- Salt and chili pepper to taste
- 3 fresh eggs
- 2 zucchinis, cut into strips
- Aioli:
- ½ cup mayonnaise
- 1 garlic clove, minced
- Juice and zest from ½ lemon

Directions:

1. Preheat oven to 425°F and line a baking sheet with foil. Grease with cooking spray and set aside. Mix the pork rinds, paprika, parmesan cheese, salt, and chili pepper in a bowl. Beat the eggs in another bowl. Coat zucchini strips in egg, then in parmesan mixture, and arrange on the baking sheet. Grease lightly with cooking spray and bake for 15 minutes to be crispy.

2. To make the aioli, combine in a bowl mayonnaise, lemon juice, and garlic, and gently stir until everything is well incorporated. Add the lemon zest, adjust the seasoning and stir again. Cover and place in the refrigerator until ready to serve. Serve the zucchini strips with garlic aioli for dipping.

Nutrition Info:
- Info Per Servings 2g Carbs, 6g Protein, 14g Fat, 180 Calories

Cheesy Cauliflower Fritters

Servings: 4
Cooking Time: 35 Minutes
Ingredients:
- 1 pound grated cauliflower
- ½ cup Parmesan cheese
- 3 ounces chopped onion
- ½ tsp baking powder
- ½ cup almond flour
- 3 eggs
- ½ tsp lemon juice
- 2 tbsp olive oil
- ⅓ tsp salt

Directions:

1. Sprinkle the salt over the cauliflower in a bowl, and let it stand for 10 minutes. Add in the other ingredients. Mix with your hands to combine. Place a skillet over medium heat, and heat olive oil.

2. Shape fritters out of the cauliflower mixture. Fry in batches, for about 3 minutes per side.

Nutrition Info:
- Info Per Servings 3g Carbs, 4.5g Protein, 4.5g Fat, 69 Calories

Parmesan Crackers With Guacamole

Servings: 4

Cooking Time: 10 Minutes

Ingredients:

- 1 cup finely grated Parmesan cheese
- ¼ tsp sweet paprika
- ¼ tsp garlic powder
- 2 soft avocados, pitted and scooped
- 1 tomato, chopped
- Salt to taste

Directions:

1. To make the chips, preheat oven to 350°F and line a baking sheet with parchment paper.

2. Mix parmesan cheese, paprika, and garlic powder. Spoon 8 teaspoons on the baking sheet creating spaces between each mound. Flatten mounds. Bake for 5 minutes, cool, and remove to a plate.

3. To make the guacamole, mash avocado, with a fork in a bowl, add in tomato and continue to mash until mostly smooth. Season with salt. Serve crackers with guacamole.

Nutrition Info:

- Info Per Servings 2g Carbs, 10g Protein, 20g Fat, 229 Calories

Turkey Pastrami & Mascarpone Cheese Pinwheels

Servings: 4

Cooking Time: 40 Minutes

Ingredients:

- Cooking spray
- 8 oz mascarpone cheese
- 10 oz turkey pastrami, sliced
- 10 canned pepperoncini peppers, sliced and drained

Directions:

1. Lay a 12 x 12 plastic wrap on a flat surface and arrange the pastrami all over slightly overlapping each other. Spread the cheese on top of the salami layers and arrange the pepperoncini on top.

2. Hold two opposite ends of the plastic wrap and roll the pastrami. Twist both ends to tighten and refrigerate for 2 hours. Unwrap the salami roll and slice into 2-inch pinwheels. Serve.

Nutrition Info:

- Info Per Servings 0g Carbs, 13g Protein, 24g Fat, 266 Calories

Keto Caprese Salad

Servings: 2

Cooking Time: 0 Minutes

Ingredients:

- 2 roma tomatoes, sliced thinly
- 8 large fresh basil leaves
- 2 oz fresh mozzarella part-skim, sliced into ½-inch cubes
- 2 tsp balsamic vinegar
- 4 tsp extra virgin olive oil
- Pepper to taste

Directions:

1. Place tomatoes on a plate.

2. Season with pepper. Sprinkle with basil and mozzarella,

3. Drizzle balsamic vinegar and olive oil before serving.

Nutrition Info:

- Info Per Servings 4g Carbs, 7g Protein, 9g Fat, 130 Calories

Buttered Broccoli

Servings: 6
Cooking Time: 10 Minutes
Ingredients:
- 1 broccoli head, florets only
- Salt and black pepper to taste
- ¼ cup butter

Directions:
1. Place the broccoli in a pot filled with salted water and bring to a boil. Cook for about 3 minutes.
2. Melt the butter in a microwave. Drain the broccoli and transfer to a plate. Drizzle the butter over and season with some salt and pepper.

Nutrition Info:
- Info Per Servings 5.5g Carbs, 3.9g Protein, 7.8g Fat, 114 Calories

Keto "cornbread"

Servings: 8
Cooking Time: 30 Minutes
Ingredients:
- 1 ¼ cups coconut milk
- 4 eggs, beaten
- 4 tbsp baking powder
- ½ cup almond meal
- 3 tablespoons olive oil

Directions:
1. Prepare 8 x 8-inch baking dish or a black iron skillet then add shortening.
2. Put the baking dish or skillet inside the oven on 425oF and leave there for 10 minutes.
3. In a bowl, add coconut milk and eggs then mix well. Stir in the rest of the ingredients.
4. Once all ingredients are mixed, pour the mixture into the heated skillet.
5. Then cook for 15 to 20 minutes in the oven until golden brown.

Nutrition Info:
- Info Per Servings 2.6g Carbs, 5.4g Protein, 18.9g Fat, 196 Calories

Duo-cheese Chicken Bake

Servings: 6
Cooking Time: 30 Minutes
Ingredients:
- 2 tbsp olive oil
- 8 oz cream cheese
- 1 lb ground chicken
- 1 cup buffalo sauce
- 1 cup ranch dressing
- 3 cups grated yellow cheddar cheese

Directions:
1. Preheat oven to 350ºF. Lightly grease a baking sheet with a cooking spray. Warm the oil in a skillet over medium heat and brown the chicken for a couple of minutes, take off the heat, and set aside.
2. Spread cream cheese at the bottom of the baking sheet, top with chicken, pour buffalo sauce over, add ranch dressing, and sprinkle with cheddar cheese. Bake for 23 minutes until cheese has melted and golden brown on top. Remove and serve with veggie sticks or low carb crackers.

Nutrition Info:
- Info Per Servings 3g Carbs, 14g Protein, 16g Fat, 216 Calories

Basil Keto Crackers

Servings: 6
Cooking Time: 15 Minutes
Ingredients:
- 1 ¼ cups almond flour
- ½ teaspoon baking powder
- ¼ teaspoon dried basil powder
- A pinch of cayenne pepper powder
- 1 clove of garlic, minced
- What you'll need from the store cupboard:
- Salt and pepper to taste
- 3 tablespoons oil

Directions:
1. Preheat oven to 350oF and lightly grease a cookie sheet with cooking spray.
2. Mix everything in a mixing bowl to create a dough.
3. Transfer the dough on a clean and flat working surface and spread out until 2mm thick. Cut into squares.
4. Place gently in an even layer on the prepped cookie sheet. Cook for 10 minutes.
5. Cook in batches.
6. Serve and enjoy.

Nutrition Info:
- Info Per Servings 2.9g Carbs, 5.3g Protein, 19.3g Fat, 205 Calories

Roasted String Beans, Mushrooms & Tomato Plate

Servings: 4
Cooking Time: 32 Minutes
Ingredients:
- 2 cups strings beans, cut in halves
- 1 lb cremini mushrooms, quartered
- 3 tomatoes, quartered
- 2 cloves garlic, minced
- 3 tbsp olive oil
- 3 shallots, julienned
- ½ tsp dried thyme
- Salt and black pepper to season

Directions:
1. Preheat oven to 450ºF. In a bowl, mix the strings beans, mushrooms, tomatoes, garlic, olive oil, shallots, thyme, salt, and pepper. Pour the vegetables in a baking sheet and spread them all around.
2. Place the baking sheet in the oven and bake the veggies for 20 to 25 minutes.

Nutrition Info:
- Info Per Servings 6g Carbs, 6g Protein, 2g Fat, 121 Calories

Mixed Roast Vegetables

Servings: 4

Cooking Time: 40 Minutes

Ingredients:

- 1 large butternut squash, cut into chunks
- ¼ lb shallots, peeled
- 4 rutabagas, cut into chunks
- ¼ lb Brussels sprouts
- 1 sprig rosemary, chopped
- 1 sprig thyme, chopped
- 4 cloves garlic, peeled only
- 3 tbsp olive oil
- Salt and black pepper to taste

Directions:

1. Preheat the oven to 450ºF.
2. Pour the butternut squash, shallots, rutabagas, garlic cloves, and brussels sprouts in a bowl. Season with salt, pepper, olive oil, and toss them. Pour the mixture on a baking sheet and sprinkle with the chopped thyme and rosemary. Roast the vegetables for 15–20 minutes.
3. Once ready, remove and spoon into a serving bowl. Serve with oven roasted chicken thighs.

Nutrition Info:

- Info Per Servings 8g Carbs, 3g Protein, 3g Fat, 65 Calories

Asian Glazed Meatballs

Servings: 4

Cooking Time: 35 Minutes

Ingredients:

- 1-pound frozen meatballs, thawed to room temperature
- ½ cup hoisin sauce
- 1 tablespoon apricot jam
- 2 tablespoons soy sauce
- ½ teaspoon sesame oil
- 5 tbsp MCT oil or coconut oil
- 2 tbsp water

Directions:

1. Place a heavy-bottomed pot on medium-high fire and heat coconut oil.
2. Sauté meatballs until lightly browned, around 10 minutes.
3. Stir in remaining ingredients and mix well.
4. Cover and cook for 25 minutes on low fire, mixing now and then.
5. Serve and enjoy.

Nutrition Info:

- Info Per Servings 6.5g Carbs, 16.3g Protein, 51.6g Fat, 536 Calories

Baba Ganoush Eggplant Dip

Servings: 4

Cooking Time: 80 Minutes

Ingredients:

- 1 head of garlic, unpeeled
- 1 large eggplant, cut in half lengthwise
- 5 tablespoons olive oil
- Lemon juice to taste
- 2 minced garlic cloves
- What you'll need from the store cupboard:
- Pepper and salt to taste

Directions:

1. With the rack in the middle position, preheat oven to 350°F.
2. Line a baking sheet with parchment paper. Place the eggplant cut side down on the baking sheet.
3. Roast until the flesh is very tender and pulls away easily from the skin, about 1 hour depending on the eggplant's size. Let it cool.
4. Meanwhile, cut the tips off the garlic cloves. Place the cloves in a square of aluminum foil. Fold up the edges of the foil and crimp together to form a tightly sealed packet. Roast alongside the eggplant until tender, about 20 minutes. Let cool.
5. Mash the cloves by pressing with a fork.
6. With a spoon, scoop the flesh from the eggplant and place it in the bowl of a food processor. Add the mashed garlic, oil and lemon juice. Process until smooth. Season with pepper.

Nutrition Info:

- Info Per Servings 10.2g Carbs, 1.6g Protein, 17.8g Fat, 192 Calories

Cajun Spiced Pecans

Servings: 10

Cooking Time: 10 Minutes

Ingredients:

- 1-pound pecan halves
- ¼ cup butter
- 1 packet Cajun seasoning mix
- ¼ teaspoon ground cayenne pepper
- Salt and pepper to taste

Directions:

1. Place a nonstick saucepan on medium fire and melt butter.
2. Add pecans and remaining ingredients.
3. Sauté for 5 minutes.
4. Remove from fire and let it cool completely.
5. Serve and enjoy.

Nutrition Info:

- Info Per Servings 6.8g Carbs, 4.2g Protein, 37.3g Fat, 356.5 Calories

Cheesy Green Bean Crisps

Servings: 6

Cooking Time: 30 Minutes

Ingredients:

- Cooking spray
- ¼ cup shredded pecorino romano cheese
- ¼ cup pork rind crumbs
- 1 tsp garlic powder
- Salt and black pepper to taste
- 2 eggs
- 1 lb green beans, thread removed

Directions:

1. Preheat oven to 425°F and line two baking sheets with foil. Grease with cooking spray and set aside.

2. Mix the pecorino, pork rinds, garlic powder, salt, and black pepper in a bowl. Beat the eggs in another bowl. Coat green beans in eggs, then cheese mixture and arrange evenly on the baking sheets.

3. Grease lightly with cooking spray and bake for 15 minutes to be crispy. Transfer to a wire rack to cool before serving. Serve with sugar-free tomato dip.

Nutrition Info:

- Info Per Servings 3g Carbs, 5g Protein, 19g Fat, 210 Calories

Bacon Jalapeno Poppers

Servings: 8

Cooking Time: 10 Minutes

Ingredients:

- 4-ounce cream cheese
- ¼ cup cheddar cheese, shredded
- 1 teaspoon paprika
- 16 fresh jalapenos, sliced lengthwise and seeded
- 16 strips of uncured bacon, cut into half
- Salt and pepper to taste

Directions:

1. Preheat oven to 400oF.
2. In a mixing bowl, mix the cream cheese, cheddar cheese, salt, and paprika until well-combined.
3. Scoop half a teaspoon onto each half of jalapeno peppers.
4. Use a thin strip of bacon and wrap it around the cheese-filled jalapeno half.
5. Place in a single layer in a lightly greased baking sheet and roast for 10 minutes.
6. Serve and enjoy.

Nutrition Info:

- Info Per Servings 3.2g Carbs, 10.6g Protein, 18.9g Fat, 225 Calories

Air Fryer Garlic Chicken Wings

Servings: 4

Cooking Time: 25 Minutes

Ingredients:

- 16 pieces chicken wings
- ¾ cup almond flour
- 4 tablespoons minced garlic
- ¼ cup butter, melted
- 2 tablespoons Stevia powder
- Salt and pepper to taste

Directions:

1. Preheat oven to 400oF.
2. In a mixing bowl, combine the chicken wings, almond flour, Stevia powder, and garlic. Season with salt and pepper to taste.
3. Place in a lightly greased cookie sheet in an even layer and cook for 25 minutes.
4. Halfway through the cooking time, turnover chicken.
5. Once cooked, place in a bowl and drizzle with melted butter. Toss to coat.
6. Serve and enjoy.

Nutrition Info:

- Info Per Servings 7.8g Carbs, 23.7g Protein, 26.9g Fat, 365 Calories

Parsnip And Carrot Fries With Aioli

Servings: 4

Cooking Time: 40 Minutes

Ingredients:

- 4 tbsp mayonnaise
- 2 garlic cloves, minced
- Salt and black pepper to taste
- 3 tbsp lemon juice
- Parsnip and Carrots Fries:
- 6 medium parsnips, julienned
- 3 large carrots, julienned
- 2 tbsp olive oil
- 5 tbsp chopped parsley
- Salt and black pepper to taste

Directions:

1. Preheat the oven to 400ºF. Make the aioli by mixing the mayonnaise with garlic, salt, pepper, and lemon juice; then refrigerate for 30 minutes.
2. Spread the parsnip and carrots on a baking sheet. Drizzle with olive oil, sprinkle with salt, and pepper, and rub the seasoning into the veggies. Bake for 35 minutes. Remove and transfer to a plate. Garnish the vegetables with parsley and serve with the chilled aioli.

Nutrition Info:

- Info Per Servings 4.4g Carbs, 2.1g Protein, 4.1g Fat, 205 Calories

Dill Pickles With Tuna-mayo Topping

Servings: 12

Cooking Time: 40 Minutes

Ingredients:

- 18 ounces canned and drained tuna
- 6 large dill pickles
- ¼ tsp garlic powder
- ⅓ cup sugar-free mayonnaise
- 1 tbsp onion flakes

Directions:

1. Combine the mayonnaise, tuna, onion flakes, and garlic powder in a bowl. Cut the pickles in half lengthwise. Top each half with tuna mixture. Place in the fridge for 30 minutes before serving.

Nutrition Info:

- Info Per Servings 1.5g Carbs, 11g Protein, 10g Fat, 118 Calories

Stuffed Jalapeno

Servings: 4

Cooking Time: 20 Minutes

Ingredients:

- 12 jalapeno peppers, halved lengthwise and seeded
- 2-oz cream cheese softened
- 2-oz shredded cheddar cheese
- ¼ cup almond meal
- Salt and pepper to taste

Directions:

1. Spray a cookie sheet with cooking spray and preheat oven to 400oF.
2. Equally fill each jalapeno with cheddar cheese, cream cheese, and sprinkle almond meal on top. Place on a prepped baking sheet.
3. Pop in oven and bake for 20 minutes.
4. Serve and enjoy.

Nutrition Info:

- Info Per Servings 7.7g Carbs, 5.9g Protein, 13.2g Fat, 187 Calories

Vegan, Vegetable & Meatless Recipes

Lemon Grilled Veggie

Servings: 4
Cooking Time: 20 Minutes

Ingredients:

- 2/3 eggplant
- 1 zucchini
- 10 oz. cheddar cheese
- 20 black olives
- 2 oz. leafy greens
- ½ cup olive oil
- 1 lemon, the juice
- 1 cup mayonnaise
- 4 tbsp almonds
- Salt and pepper

Directions:

1. Cut eggplant and zucchini lengthwise into half inch-thick slices. Season with salt to coat evenly. Set aside for 5-10 minutes.
2. Preheat the oven to 450 degrees F.
3. Pat zucchini and eggplant slices' surface dry with a kitchen towel.
4. Line a baking sheet with parchment paper and place slices on it. Spray with olive oil on top and season with pepper.
5. Bake for 15-20 minutes or until cooked through, flipping halfway.
6. Once done, transfer to a serving platter. Drizzle olive oil and lemon juice on top.
7. Serve with cheese cubes, almonds, olives, mayonnaise and leafy greens.

Nutrition Info:

- Info Per Servings 9g Carbs, 21g Protein, 99g Fat, 1013 Calories

Sriracha Tofu With Yogurt Sauce

Servings: 4
Cooking Time: 40 Minutes

Ingredients:

- 12 ounces tofu, pressed and sliced
- 1 cup green onions, chopped
- 1 garlic clove, minced
- 2 tbsp vinegar
- 1 tbsp sriracha sauce
- 2 tbsp olive oil
- For Yogurt Sauce
- 2 cloves garlic, pressed
- 2 tbsp fresh lemon juice
- Sea salt and black pepper, to taste
- 1 tsp fresh dill weed
- 1 cup Greek yogurt
- 1 cucumber, shredded

Directions:

1. Put tofu slices, garlic, Sriracha sauce, vinegar, and scallions in a bowl; allow to settle for approximately 30 minutes. Set oven to medium-high heat and add oil in a nonstick skillet to warm. Cook tofu for 5 minutes until golden brown.

2. For the preparation of sauce, use a bowl to mix garlic, salt, yogurt, black pepper, lemon juice, and dill. Add in shredded cucumber as you stir to combine well. Put the yogurt sauce in your fridge until ready to serve. Serve the tofu in serving plates with a dollop of yogurt sauce.

Nutrition Info:

- Info Per Servings 8.1g Carbs, 17.5g Protein, 25.9g Fat, 351 Calories

Vegetable Greek Mousaka

Servings: 6
Cooking Time: 50 Minutes
Ingredients:

- 2 large eggplants, cut into strips
- 1 cup diced celery
- 1 cup diced carrots
- 1 small white onion, chopped
- 2 eggs
- 1 tsp olive oil
- 3 cups grated Parmesan, divided into 2
- 1 cup ricotta cheese
- 3 cloves garlic, minced
- 2 tsp Italian seasoning blend
- Salt to taste
- Sauce:
- 1 ½ cups heavy cream
- ¼ cup butter, melted
- 1 cup grated mozzarella cheese
- 2 tsp Italian seasoning
- ¾ cup almond flour

Directions:

1. Preheat the oven to 350°F. Lay the eggplant strips on a paper towel, sprinkle with salt and let sit there to exude liquid. Heat olive oil in a skillet over medium heat and sauté the onion, celery, and carrots for 5 minutes. Stir in the garlic and cook further for 30 seconds; set aside to cool.

2. Mix the eggs, 1 cup of parmesan cheese, ricotta cheese, and salt in a bowl; set aside. Pour the heavy cream in a pot and bring to heat over a medium fire while continually stirring. Stir in the remaining parmesan cheese, and 1 teaspoon of Italian seasoning. Turn the heat off and set aside.

3. To lay the mousaka, spread a small amount of the sauce at the bottom of the baking dish. Pat dry the eggplant strips and make a single layer on the sauce. Spread a layer of ricotta cheese on the eggplants, sprinkle some veggies on it, and repeat the layering process from the sauce until all the ingredients are exhausted.

4. In a small bowl, evenly mix the melted butter, almond flour, and 1 teaspoon of Italian seasoning. Spread the top of the mousaka layers with it and sprinkle the top with mozzarella cheese. Cover the dish with foil and place it in the oven to bake for 25 minutes. Remove the foil and bake for 5 minutes until the cheese is slightly burned. Slice the mousaka and serve warm.

Nutrition Info:

- Info Per Servings 9.6g Carbs, 33g Protein, 35g Fat, 476 Calories

Cream Of Zucchini And Avocado

Servings: 4
Cooking Time: 35 Minutes
Ingredients:

- 3 tsp vegetable oil
- 1 onion, chopped
- 1 carrot, sliced
- 1 turnip, sliced
- 3 cups zucchinis, chopped
- 1 avocado, peeled and diced
- ¼ tsp ground black pepper
- 4 vegetable broth
- 1 tomato, pureed

Directions:

1. In a pot, warm the oil and sauté onion until translucent, about 3 minutes. Add in turnip, zucchini, and carrot and cook for 7 minutes; add black pepper for seasoning.

2. Mix in pureed tomato, and broth; and boil. Change heat to low and allow the mixture to simmer for 20 minutes. Lift from the heat. In batches, add the soup and avocado to a blender. Blend until creamy and smooth.

Nutrition Info:

- Info Per Servings 11g Carbs, 2.2g Protein, 13.4g Fat, 165 Calories

Walnut Tofu Sauté

Servings: 4
Cooking Time: 15 Minutes
Ingredients:

- 1 tbsp olive oil
- 1 block firm tofu, cubed
- 1 tbsp tomato paste with garlic and onion
- 1 tbsp balsamic vinegar
- Pink salt and black pepper to taste
- ½ tsp mixed dried herbs
- 1 cup chopped raw walnuts

Directions:

1. Heat the oil in a skillet over medium heat and cook the tofu for 3 minutes while stirring to brown.
2. Mix the tomato paste with the vinegar and add to the tofu. Stir, season with salt and black pepper, and cook for another 4 minutes.
3. Add the herbs and walnuts. Stir and cook on low heat for 3 minutes to be fragrant. Spoon to a side of squash mash and a sweet berry sauce to serve.

Nutrition Info:

- Info Per Servings 4g Carbs, 18g Protein, 24g Fat, 320 Calories

Grilled Spicy Eggplant

Servings: 2
Cooking Time: 20 Minutes
Ingredients:

- 2 small eggplants, cut into 1/2-inch slices
- 1/4 cup olive oil
- 2 tablespoons lime juice
- 3 teaspoons Cajun seasoning
- Salt and pepper to taste

Directions:

1. Brush eggplant slices with oil. Drizzle with lime juice; sprinkle with Cajun seasoning. Let stand for 5 minutes.
2. Grill eggplant, covered, over medium heat or broil 4 minutes. from heat until tender, 4-5 minutes per side.
3. Season with pepper and salt to taste.
4. Serve and enjoy.

Nutrition Info:

- Info Per Servings 7g Carbs, 5g Protein, 28g Fat, 350 Calories

Butternut Squash And Cauliflower Stew

Servings: 4
Cooking Time:10 Minutes
Ingredients:

- 3 cloves of garlic, minced
- 1 cup cauliflower florets
- 1 ½ cups butternut squash, cubed
- 2 ½ cups heavy cream
- Pepper and salt to taste
- 3 tbsp coconut oil

Directions:

1. Heat the oil in a pan and saute the garlic until fragrant.
2. Stir in the rest of the ingredients and season with salt and pepper to taste.
3. Close the lid and bring to a boil for 10 minutes.
4. Serve and enjoy.

Nutrition Info:

- Info Per Servings 10g Carbs, 2g Protein, 38.1g Fat, 385 Calories

Crispy-topped Baked Vegetables

Servings: 4
Cooking Time: 40 Minutes
Ingredients:

- 2 tbsp olive oil
- 1 onion, chopped
- 1 celery, chopped
- 2 carrots, grated
- ½ pound turnip, sliced
- 1 cup vegetable broth
- 1 tsp turmeric
- Sea salt and black pepper, to taste
- ½ tsp liquid smoke
- 1 cup Parmesan cheese, shredded
- 2 tbsp fresh chives, chopped

Directions:

1. Set oven to 360ºF. Grease a baking dish with olive oil. Set a skillet over medium-high heat and warm olive oil. Sweat the onion until soft. Place in the turnip slices and celery. Cook for 4 minutes.

2. Remove the vegetable mixture to the baking dish. Combine vegetable broth with turmeric, black pepper, liquid smoke, and salt.

3. Spread this mixture over the vegetables. Apply a topping of vegan parmesan cheese and bake for about 30 minutes. Decorate with fresh chives and serve.

Nutrition Info:

- Info Per Servings 8.6g Carbs, 16.3g Protein, 16.3g Fat, 242 Calories

Vegetable Tempura

Servings: 4
Cooking Time: 17 Minutes
Ingredients:

- ½ cup coconut flour + extra for dredging
- Salt and black pepper to taste
- 3 egg yolks
- 2 red bell peppers, cut into strips
- 1 squash, peeled and cut into strips
- 1 broccoli, cut into florets
- 1 cup Chilled water
- Olive oil for frying
- Lemon wedges to serve
- Sugar-free soy sauce to serve

Directions:

1. In a deep frying pan or wok, heat the olive oil over medium heat. Beat the eggs lightly with ½ cup of coconut flour and water. The mixture should be lumpy. Dredge the vegetables lightly in some flour, shake off the excess flour, dip it in the batter, and then into the hot oil.

2. Fry in batches for 1 minute each, not more, and remove with a perforated spoon onto a wire rack. Sprinkle with salt and pepper and serve with the lemon wedges and soy sauce.

Nutrition Info:

- Info Per Servings 0.9g Carbs, 3g Protein, 17g Fat, 218 Calories

Coconut Cauliflower & Parsnip Soup

Servings: 4

Cooking Time: 20 Minutes

Ingredients:

- 4 cups vegetable broth
- 2 heads cauliflower, cut into florets
- 1 cup parsnip, chopped
- 1 tbsp coconut oil
- 1 cup coconut milk
- ½ tsp red pepper flakes

Directions:

1. Add water in a pot set over medium-high heat and bring to a boil. Add in cauliflower florets and parsnip, cook for about 10 minutes. Add in broth and coconut oil. While on low heat, cook for an additional 5 minutes. Transfer the mixture to an immersion blender and puree.
2. Plate into four separate soup bowls; decorate each with red pepper flakes. Serve while warm.

Nutrition Info:

- Info Per Servings 7g Carbs, 2.7g Protein, 7.2g Fat, 94 Calories

Stuffed Cremini Mushrooms

Servings: 4

Cooking Time: 35 Minutes

Ingredients:

- ½ head broccoli, cut into florets
- 1 pound cremini mushrooms, stems removed
- 2 tbsp coconut oil
- 1 onion, finely chopped
- 1 tsp garlic, minced
- 1 bell pepper, chopped
- 1 tsp cajun seasoning mix
- Salt and black pepper, to taste
- 1 cup vegan cheese

Directions:

1. Use a food processor to pulse broccoli florets until become like small rice-like granules.
2. Set oven to 360ºF. Bake mushroom caps until tender for 8 to 12 minutes. In a heavy-bottomed skillet, melt the oil; stir in bell pepper, garlic, and onion and sauté until fragrant. Place in pepper, salt, and cajun seasoning mix. Fold in broccoli rice.
3. Equally separate the filling mixture among mushroom caps. Add a topping of vegan cheese and bake for 17 more minutes. Serve warm.

Nutrition Info:

- Info Per Servings 10g Carbs, 12.7g Protein, 13.4g Fat, 206 Calories

Kale Cheese Waffles

Servings: 4
Cooking Time: 45 Minutes
Ingredients:

- 2 green onions
- 1 tbsp olive oil
- 2 eggs
- ⅓ cup Parmesan cheese
- 1 cup kale, chopped

- 1 cup mozzarella cheese
- ½ cauliflower head
- 1 tsp garlic powder
- 1 tbsp sesame seeds
- 2 tsp chopped thyme

Directions:

1. Place the chopped cauliflower in the food processor and process until rice is formed. Add kale, spring onions, and thyme to the food processor. Pulse until smooth. Transfer to a bowl. Stir in the rest of the ingredients and mix to combine.
2. Heat waffle iron and spread in the mixture, evenly. Cook following the manufacturer's instructions.

Nutrition Info:

- Info Per Servings 3.6g Carbs, 16g Protein, 20.2g Fat, 283 Calories

Avocado And Tomato Burritos

Servings: 4
Cooking Time: 5 Minutes
Ingredients:

- 2 cups cauli rice
- Water for sprinkling
- 6 zero carb flatbread

- 2 cups sour cream sauce
- 1 ½ cups tomato herb salsa
- 2 avocados, peeled, pitted, sliced

Directions:

1. Pour the cauli rice in a bowl, sprinkle with water, and soften in the microwave for 2 minutes.
2. On flatbread, spread the sour cream all over and distribute the salsa on top. Top with cauli rice and scatter the avocado evenly on top. Fold and tuck the burritos and cut into two.

Nutrition Info:

- Info Per Servings 6g Carbs, 8g Protein, 25g Fat, 303 Calories

Vegetable Burritos

Servings: 4
Cooking Time: 10 Minutes
Ingredients:

- 2 large low carb tortillas
- 2 tsp olive oil
- 1 small onion, sliced
- 1 bell pepper, seeded and sliced
- 1 large ripe avocado, pitted and sliced

- 1 cup lemon cauli couscous
- Salt and black pepper to taste
- ⅓ cup sour cream
- 3 tbsp Mexican salsa

Directions:

1. Heat the olive oil in a skillet and sauté the onion and bell pepper until they start to brown on the edges, about 4 minutes. Turn the heat off and set the skillet aside.
2. Lay the tortillas on a flat surface and top each with halves of the onion and bell pepper mixture, avocado, cauli couscous, season with salt and pepper, sour cream, and Mexican salsa. Fold in the sides of each tortilla, and roll them in and over the filling to be completely enclosed.
3. Wrap with foil, cut in halves, and serve warm.

Nutrition Info:

- Info Per Servings 5.4g Carbs, 17.9g Protein, 23.2g Fat, 373 Calories

Guacamole

Servings: 2

Cooking Time: 0 Minutes

Ingredients:

- 2 medium ripe avocados
- 1 tablespoon lemon juice
- 1/4 cup chopped tomatoes
- 4 tablespoons olive oil
- 1/4 teaspoon salt
- Pepper to taste

Directions:

1. Peel and chop avocados; place them in a small bowl. Sprinkle with lemon juice.
2. Add tomatoes and salt.
3. Season with pepper to taste and mash coarsely with a fork. Refrigerate until serving.

Nutrition Info:

- Info Per Servings 10g Carbs, 6g Protein, 56g Fat, 565 Calories

Tomato Stuffed Avocado

Servings: 4

Cooking Time: 10 Minutes

Ingredients:

- 2 avocados, peeled and pitted
- 1 tomato, chopped
- ¼ cup walnuts, ground
- 2 carrots, chopped
- 1 garlic clove
- 1 tsp lemon juice
- 1 tbsp soy sauce
- Salt and black pepper, to taste

Directions:

1. Using a mixing bowl, mix soy sauce, carrots, avocado pulp, lemon juice, walnuts, and garlic.
2. Add pepper and salt. Plate the mixture into the avocado halves. Scatter walnuts over to serve.

Nutrition Info:

- Info Per Servings 5.5g Carbs, 3.5g Protein, 24.8g Fat, 263 Calories

Vegetarian Burgers

Servings: 2

Cooking Time: 20 Minutes

Ingredients:

- 1 garlic cloves, minced
- 2 portobello mushrooms, sliced
- 1 tbsp coconut oil, melted
- 1 tbsp chopped basil
- 1 tbsp oregano
- 2 eggs, fried
- 2 low carb buns
- 2 tbsp mayonnaise
- 2 lettuce leaves

Directions:

1. Combine the melted coconut oil, garlic, herbs, and salt, in a bowl. Place the mushrooms in the bowl and coat well. Preheat the grill to medium heat. Grill the mushrooms for 2 minutes per side.

2. Cut the low carb buns in half. Add the lettuce leaves, grilled mushrooms, eggs, and mayonnaise. Top with the other bun half.

Nutrition Info:

- Info Per Servings 8.5g Carbs, 23g Protein, 55g Fat, 637 Calories

Creamy Almond And Turnip Soup

Servings: 4

Cooking Time: 25 Minutes

Ingredients:

- 1 tbsp olive oil
- 1 cup onion, chopped
- 1 celery, chopped
- 2 cloves garlic, minced
- 2 turnips, peeled and chopped
- 4 cups vegetable broth
- Salt and white pepper, to taste
- ¼ cup ground almonds
- 1 cup almond milk
- 1 tbsp fresh cilantro, chopped

Directions:

1. Set a stockpot over medium-high heat and warm the oil. Add in celery, garlic, and onion and sauté for 6 minutes. Stir in white pepper, broth, salt, and ground almonds. Boil the mixture. Set heat to low and simmer for 17 minutes. Transfer the soup to an immersion blender and puree. Decorate with fresh cilantro before serving.

Nutrition Info:

- Info Per Servings 9.2g Carbs, 3.8g Protein, 6.5g Fat, 114 Calories

Tasty Cauliflower Dip

Servings: 4

Cooking Time: 10 Minutes

Ingredients:

- ¾ pound cauliflower, cut into florets
- ¼ cup olive oil
- Salt and black pepper, to taste
- 1 garlic clove, smashed
- 1 tbsp sesame paste
- 1 tbsp fresh lime juice
- ½ tsp garam masala

Directions:

1. Steam cauliflower until tender for 7 minutes in. Transfer to a blender and pulse until you attain a rice-like consistency.

2. Place in Garam Masala, oil, black paper, fresh lime juice, garlic, salt, and sesame paste. Blend the mixture until well combined. Decorate with some additional olive oil and serve. Otherwise, refrigerate until ready to use.

Nutrition Info:

- Info Per Servings 4.7g Carbs, 3.7g Protein, 8.2g Fat, 100 Calories

Keto Pizza Margherita

Servings: 2
Cooking Time: 40 Minutes
Ingredients:

- 6 ounces mozzarella
- 2 tbsp cream cheese
- 2 tbsp Parmesan cheese
- 1 tsp oregano
- ½ cup almond flour
- 2 tbsp psyllium husk
- Topping
- 4 ounces grated cheddar cheese
- ¼ cup Marinara sauce
- 1 bell pepper, sliced
- 1 tomato, sliced
- 2 tbsp chopped basil

Directions:

1. Preheat the oven to 400ºF. Combine all crust ingredients in a large bowl, except the mozzarella.
2. Melt the mozzarella in a microwave. Stir it into the bowl. Mix with your hands to combine. Divide the dough in two. Roll out the two crusts in circles and place on a lined baking sheet. Bake for about 10 minutes. Top with the toppings. Return to the oven and bake for another 10 minutes.

Nutrition Info:

- Info Per Servings 3.7g Carbs, 31g Protein, 39g Fat, 510 Calories

Cilantro-lime Guacamole

Servings: 4
Cooking Time: 10 Minutes
Ingredients:

- 3 avocados, peeled, pitted, and mashed
- 1 lime, juiced
- 1/2 cup diced onion
- 3 tablespoons chopped fresh cilantro
- 2 Roma (plum) tomatoes, diced
- 1 teaspoon salt
- 1 teaspoon minced garlic
- 1 pinch ground cayenne pepper (optional)
- 1 teaspoon minced garlic

Directions:

1. In a mixing bowl, mash the avocados with a fork. Sprinkle with salt and lime juice.
2. Stir together diced onion, tomatoes, cilantro, pepper and garlic.
3. Serve immediately, or refrigerate until ready to serve.

Nutrition Info:

- Info Per Servings 8g Carbs, 19g Protein, 22.2g Fat, 362 Calories

Garlic And Greens

Servings: 4
Cooking Time: 20 Minutes
Ingredients:

- 1-pound kale, trimmed and torn
- 1/4 cup chopped oil-packed sun-dried tomatoes
- 5 garlic cloves, minced
- 2 tablespoons minced fresh parsley
- 1/4 teaspoon salt
- 3 tablespoons olive oil

Directions:

1. In a 6-qt. stockpot, bring 1 inch. of water to a boil. Add kale; cook, covered, 10-15 minutes or until tender. Remove with a slotted spoon; discard cooking liquid.
2. In the same pot, heat oil over medium heat. Add tomatoes and garlic; cook and stir 1 minute. Add kale, parsley and salt; heat through, stirring occasionally.

Nutrition Info:

- Info Per Servings 9g Carbs, 6g Protein, 13g Fat, 160 Calories

Poultry Recipes

Red Wine Chicken

Servings: 4
Cooking Time: 30 Minutes
Ingredients:

- 3 tbsp coconut oil
- 2 lb chicken breast halves, skinless and boneless
- 3 garlic cloves, minced
- Salt and black pepper, to taste
- 1 cup chicken stock
- 3 tbsp stevia
- ½ cup red wine
- 2 tomatoes, sliced
- 6 mozzarella slices
- Fresh basil, chopped, for serving

Directions:

1. Set a pan over medium-high heat and warm oil, add the chicken, season with pepper and salt, cook until brown. Stir in the stevia, garlic, stock, and red wine, and cook for 10 minutes.
2. Remove to a lined baking sheet and arrange mozzarella cheese slices on top. Broil in the oven over medium heat until cheese melts and lay tomato slices over chicken pieces.
3. Sprinkle with chopped basil to serve.

Nutrition Info:

- Info Per Servings 4g Carbs, 27g Protein, 12g Fat, 314 Calories

Grilled Paprika Chicken With Steamed Broccoli

Servings: 6
Cooking Time: 17 Minutes
Ingredients:

- Cooking spray
- 3 tbsp smoked paprika
- Salt and black pepper to taste
- 2 tsp garlic powder
- 1 tbsp olive oil
- 6 chicken breasts
- 1 head broccoli, cut into florets

Directions:

1. Place broccoli florets onto the steamer basket over the boiling water; steam approximately 8 minutes or until crisp-tender. Set aside. Grease grill grate with cooking spray and preheat to 400°F.
2. Combine paprika, salt, black pepper, and garlic powder in a bowl. Brush chicken with olive oil and sprinkle spice mixture over and massage with hands.
3. Grill chicken for 7 minutes per side until well-cooked, and plate. Serve warm with steamed broccoli.

Nutrition Info:

- Info Per Servings 2g Carbs, 26g Protein, 35.3g Fat, 422 Calories

Habanero Chicken Wings

Servings: 4
Cooking Time: 65 Minutes
Ingredients:

- 2 pounds chicken wings
- Salt and black pepper, to taste
- 3 tbsp coconut aminos
- 2 tsp white vinegar
- 3 tbsp rice vinegar
- 3 tbsp stevia
- ¼ cup chives, chopped
- ½ tsp xanthan gum
- 5 dried habanero peppers, chopped

Directions:

1. Spread the chicken wings on a lined baking sheet, sprinkle with pepper and salt, set in an oven at 370ºF, and bake for 45 minutes. Put a small pan over medium heat, add in the white vinegar, coconut aminos, chives, stevia, rice vinegar, xanthan gum, and habanero peppers, bring the mixture to a boil, cook for 2 minutes, and remove from heat.

2. Dip the chicken wings into this sauce, lay them all on the baking sheet again, and bake for 10 more minutes. Serve warm.

Nutrition Info:

- Info Per Servings 2g Carbs, 26g Protein, 25g Fat, 416 Calories

Duck & Vegetable Casserole

Servings: 2
Cooking Time: 20 Minutes
Ingredients:

- 2 duck breasts, skin on and sliced
- 2 zucchinis, sliced
- 1 tbsp coconut oil
- 1 green onion bunch, chopped
- 1 carrot, chopped
- 2 green bell peppers, seeded and chopped
- Salt and ground black pepper, to taste

Directions:

1. Set a pan over medium-high heat and warm oil, stir in the green onions, and cook for 2 minutes. Place in the zucchini, bell peppers, pepper, salt, and carrot, and cook for 10 minutes.

2. Set another pan over medium-high heat, add in duck slices and cook each side for 3 minutes. Pour the mixture into the vegetable pan. Cook for 3 minutes. Set in bowls and enjoy.

Nutrition Info:

- Info Per Servings 8g Carbs, 53g Protein, 21g Fat, 433 Calories

Garlic & Ginger Chicken With Peanut Sauce

Servings: 6

Cooking Time: 1 Hour And 50 Minutes

Ingredients:

- 1 tbsp wheat-free soy sauce
- 1 tbsp sugar-free fish sauce
- 1 tbsp lime juice
- 1 tsp cilantro
- 1 tsp minced garlic
- 1 tsp minced ginger
- 1 tbsp olive oil
- 1 tbsp rice wine vinegar
- 1 tsp cayenne pepper
- 1 tsp erythritol
- 6 chicken thighs

- Sauce:
- ½ cup peanut butter
- 1 tsp minced garlic
- 1 tbsp lime juice
- 2 tbsp water
- 1 tsp minced ginger
- 1 tbsp chopped jalapeño
- 2 tbsp rice wine vinegar
- 2 tbsp erythritol
- 1 tbsp fish sauce

Directions:

1. Combine all chicken ingredients in a large Ziploc bag. Seal the bag and shake to combine. Refrigerate for 1 hour. Remove from fridge about 15 minutes before cooking.

2. Preheat the grill to medium and grill the chicken for 7 minutes per side. Whisk together all sauce ingredients in a mixing bowl. Serve the chicken drizzled with peanut sauce.

Nutrition Info:

- Info Per Servings 3g Carbs, 35g Protein, 36g Fat, 492 Calories

One Pot Chicken With Mushrooms

Servings: 6

Cooking Time: 35 Minutes

Ingredients:

- 2 cups sliced mushrooms
- ½ tsp onion powder
- ½ tsp garlic powder
- ¼ cup butter
- 1 tsp Dijon mustard
- 1 tbsp tarragon, chopped
- 2 pounds chicken thighs
- Salt and black pepper, to taste

Directions:

1. Season the thighs with salt, pepper, garlic, and onion powder. Melt the butter in a skillet, and cook the chicken until browned; set aside. Add mushrooms to the same fat and cook for about 5 minutes.

2. Stir in Dijon mustard and ½ cup of water. Return the chicken to the skillet. Season to taste with salt and pepper, reduce the heat and cover, and let simmer for 15 minutes. Stir in tarragon. Serve warm.

Nutrition Info:

- Info Per Servings 1g Carbs, 31g Protein, 37g Fat, 447 Calories

Marinara Chicken Sausage

Servings: 6
Cooking Time: 40 Minutes
Ingredients:

- 1-pound Italian chicken sausage
- 1 bell pepper, chopped
- 1 jar marinara sauce
- 1 cup mozzarella cheese, grated
- 4 tablespoons oil
- Salt and pepper to taste
- ¼ cup water

Directions:

1. Place a heavy-bottomed pot on medium-high fire and heat for 2 minutes. Add oil and swirl to coat the bottom and sides of pot and heat for a minute.
2. Sauté Italian chicken sausage for 5 minutes. Transfer to a chopping board and slice.
3. In the same pot, add marinara sauce, water, bell pepper, and sliced sausage. Cover and simmer for 30 minutes. Stir the bottom of the pot every now and then. Adjust seasoning to taste.
4. Top with marinara sauce.
5. Sprinkle top with pepper, serve, and enjoy.

Nutrition Info:

- Info Per Servings 4.4g Carbs, 33.9g Protein, 23.4g Fat, 402 Calories

Pacific Chicken

Servings: 6
Cooking Time: 50 Minutes
Ingredients:

- 4 chicken breasts
- Salt and black pepper, to taste
- ½ cup mayonnaise
- 3 tbsp Dijon mustard
- 1 tsp xylitol
- ¾ cup pork rinds
- ¾ cup grated Grana-Padano cheese
- 2 tsp garlic powder
- 1 tsp onion powder
- ¼ tsp salt
- ¼ tsp black pepper
- 8 pieces ham, sliced
- 4 slices gruyere cheese

Directions:

1. Set an oven to 350°F and grease a baking dish. Using a small bowl, place in the pork rinds and crush. Add chicken to a plate and season well.
2. In a separate bowl, mix mustard, mayonnaise, and xylitol. Take about ¼ of this mixture and spread over the chicken. Preserve the rest. Take ½ pork rinds, seasonings, most of Grana-Padano cheese, and place to the bottom of the baking dish. Add the chicken to the top.
3. Cover the chicken with the remaining Grana-Padano, pork rinds, and seasonings. Place in the oven for about 40 minutes until the chicken is cooked completely. Take out from the oven and top with gruyere cheese and ham. Place back in the oven and cook until golden brown.

Nutrition Info:

- Info Per Servings 2.6g Carbs, 33g Protein, 31g Fat, 465 Calories

Avocado Cheese Pepper Chicken

Servings: 5
Cooking Time: 20 Minutes
Ingredients:

- ¼ tsp. cayenne pepper
- 1½ cup. cooked and shredded chicken
- 2 tbsps. cream cheese
- 2 tbsps. lemon juice
- 2 large avocados, diced
- Black pepper and salt to taste
- ¼ cup. mayonnaise
- 1 tsp. dried thyme
- ½ tsp. onion powder
- ½ tsp. garlic powder

Directions:

1. Remove the insides of your avocado halves and set them in a bowl.
2. Stir all ingredients to avocado flesh.
3. Fill avocados with chicken mix.
4. Serve and enjoy.

Nutrition Info:

- Info Per Servings 5g Carbs, 24g Protein, 40g Fat, 476 Calories

Chicken In White Wine Sauce

Servings: 4
Cooking Time: 50 Minutes
Ingredients:

- 8 chicken thighs
- Salt and black pepper, to taste
- 1 onion, peeled and chopped
- 1 tbsp coconut oil
- 4 pancetta strips, chopped
- 4 garlic cloves, minced
- 10 oz white mushrooms, halved
- 2 cups white wine
- 1 cup whipping cream
- ½ cup fresh parsley, chopped

Directions:

1. Set a pan over medium heat and warm oil, cook the pancetta until crispy, about 4-5 minutes and remove to paper towels. To the pancetta fat, add the chicken, sprinkle with pepper and salt, cook until brown, and remove to paper towels too.
2. In the same pan, sauté the onion and garlic for 4 minutes. Then, mix in the mushrooms and cook for another 5 minutes. Return the pancetta and browned chicken to the pan.
3. Stir in the wine and bring to a boil, reduce the heat, and simmer for 20 minutes. Pour in the whipping cream and warm without boiling. Split among serving bowls and enjoy. Scatter over the parsley and serve with steamed green beans.

Nutrition Info:

- Info Per Servings 4g Carbs, 24g Protein, 12g Fat, 345 Calories

Chicken Cauliflower Bake

Servings: 6
Cooking Time: 58 Minutes
Ingredients:

- 3 cups cubed leftover chicken
- 3 cups spinach
- 2 cauliflower heads, cut into florets
- 3 cups water
- 3 eggs, lightly beaten
- 2 cups grated sharp cheddar cheese
- 1 cup pork rinds, crushed
- ½ cup unsweetened almond milk
- 3 tbsp olive oil
- 3 cloves garlic, minced
- Salt and black pepper to taste
- Cooking spray

Directions:

1. Preheat the oven to 350ºF and grease a baking dish with cooking spray. Set aside.
2. Then, pour the cauli florets and water in a pot; bring to boil over medium heat. Cover and steam the cauli florets for 8 minutes. After, drain them through a colander and set aside.
3. Also, combine the cheddar cheese and pork rinds in a large bowl and mix in the chicken. Set aside.
4. Next, heat the olive oil in a large skillet and cook the garlic and spinach until the spinach has wilted, about 5 minutes. Season with salt and pepper, and add the spinach mixture and cauli florets to the chicken bowl.
5. Top with the eggs and almond milk, mix and transfer everything to the baking dish. Layer the top of the ingredients and place the dish in the oven to bake for 30 minutes.
6. By this time the edges and top must have browned nicely, then remove the chicken from the oven, let rest for 5 minutes, and serve. Garnish with steamed and seasoned green beans.

Nutrition Info:

- Info Per Servings 3g Carbs, 22g Protein, 27g Fat, 390 Calories

Coconut Chicken Soup

Servings: 4
Cooking Time: 30 Minutes
Ingredients:

- 3 tbsp butter
- 4 ounces cream cheese
- 2 chicken breasts, diced
- 4 cups chicken stock
- Salt and black pepper, to taste
- ½ cup coconut cream
- ¼ cup celery, chopped

Directions:

1. In the blender, combine stock, butter, coconut cream, salt, cream cheese, and pepper. Remove to a pot, heat over medium heat, and stir in the chicken and celery. Simmer for 15 minutes, separate into bowls, and enjoy.

Nutrition Info:

- Info Per Servings 5g Carbs, 31g Protein, 23g Fat, 387 Calories

Chicken In Creamy Spinach Sauce

Servings: 4
Cooking Time: 20 Minutes
Ingredients:

- 1 pound chicken thighs
- 2 tbsp coconut oil
- 2 tbsp coconut flour
- 2 cups spinach, chopped
- 1 tsp oregano
- 1 cup heavy cream
- 1 cup chicken broth
- 2 tbsp butter

Directions:

1. Warm the coconut oil in a skillet and brown the chicken on all sides, about 6-8 minutes. Set aside.
2. Melt the butter and whisk in the flour over medium heat. Whisk in the heavy cream and chicken broth and bring to a boil. Stir in oregano. Add the spinach to the skillet and cook until wilted.
3. Add the thighs in the skillet and cook for an additional 5 minutes.

Nutrition Info:

- Info Per Servings 2.6g Carbs, 18g Protein, 38g Fat, 446 Calories

Chicken Cacciatore

Servings: 6
Cooking Time: 35 Minutes
Ingredients:

- 6 chicken drumsticks, bone-in
- 1 bay leaf
- 4 roma tomatoes, chopped
- ½ cup black olives, pitted
- 3 cloves garlic, minced
- Salt and pepper to taste
- 1 cup water
- 1 tsp oil

Directions:

1. On high fire, heat a saucepan for 2 minutes. Add oil to the pan and swirl to coat bottom and sides. Heat oil for a minute.
2. Add garlic and sauté for a minute. Stir in tomatoes and bay leaf. Crumble and wilt tomatoes for 5 minutes.
3. Add chicken and continue sautéing for 7 minutes.
4. Deglaze the pot with ½ cup water.
5. Add remaining ingredients. Season generously with salt and pepper.
6. Lower fire to low, cover, and simmer for 20 minutes.
7. Serve and enjoy.

Nutrition Info:

- Info Per Servings 9.5g Carbs, 25.3g Protein, 13.2g Fat, 256 Calories

Chicken Drumsticks In Tomato Sauce

Servings: 4

Cooking Time: 1 Hour 35 Minutes

Ingredients:

- 8 chicken drumsticks
- 1 ½ tbsp olive oil
- 1 medium white onion, diced
- 3 medium turnips, peeled and diced
- 2 medium carrots, chopped in 1-inch pieces
- 2 green bell peppers, seeded, cut into chunks
- 2 cloves garlic, minced
- ¼ cup coconut flour
- 1 cup chicken broth
- 1 can sugar-free tomato sauce
- 2 tbsp dried Italian herbs
- Salt and black pepper to taste

Directions:

1. Preheat oven to 400ºF.
2. Heat the oil in a large skillet over medium heat, meanwhile season the drumsticks with salt and pepper, and fry them in the oil to brown on both sides for 10 minutes. Remove to a baking dish.
3. Next, sauté the onion, turnips, bell peppers, carrots, and garlic in the same oil and for 10 minutes with continuous stirring.
4. Then, in a bowl, evenly combine the broth, coconut flour, tomato paste, and Italian herbs together, and pour it over the vegetables in the pan. Stir and cook to thicken for 4 minutes.
5. Turn the heat off and pour the mixture on the chicken in the baking dish. Bake the chicken and vegetables in the oven for around 1 hour. Remove from the oven and serve with steamed cauli rice.

Nutrition Info:

- Info Per Servings 7.3g Carbs, 50.8g Protein, 34.2g Fat, 515 Calories

Rosemary Grilled Chicken

Servings: 4

Cooking Time: 12 Minutes

Ingredients:

- 1 tablespoon fresh parsley, finely chopped
- 1 tablespoon fresh rosemary, finely chopped
- 4 tablespoons olive oil
- 4 pieces of 4-oz chicken breast, boneless and skinless
- 5 cloves garlic, minced
- Pepper and salt to taste

Directions:

1. In a shallow and large bowl, mix salt, parsley, rosemary, olive oil, and garlic. Place chicken breast and marinate in the bowl of herbs for at least an hour or more before grilling.
2. Grease grill, grate and preheat grill to medium-high fire. Once hot, grill chicken for 4 to 5 minutes per side or until juices run a clear and internal temperature of chicken is 168oF.

Nutrition Info:

- Info Per Servings 1.0g Carbs, 34.0g Protein, 16.0g Fat, 238 Calories

Chicken With Green Sauce

Servings: 4
Cooking Time: 35 Minutes
Ingredients:

- 2 tbsp butter
- 4 scallions, chopped
- 4 chicken breasts, skinless and boneless
- Salt and black pepper, to taste
- 6 ounces sour cream
- 2 tbsp fresh dill, chopped

Directions:

1. Heat a pan with the butter over medium-high heat, add in the chicken, season with pepper and salt, and fry for 2-3 per side until golden. Transfer to a baking dish and cook in the oven for 15 minutes at 390°F, until no longer pink.
2. To the pan add scallions, and cook for 2 minutes. Pour in the sour cream, warm through without boil. Slice the chicken and serve on a platter with green sauce spooned over and fresh dill.

Nutrition Info:

- Info Per Servings 2.3g Carbs, 18g Protein, 9g Fat, 236 Calories

Chicken And Mushrooms

Servings: 6
Cooking Time: 30 Minutes
Ingredients:

- 6 boneless chicken breasts, halved
- 1 onion, chopped
- 4 cloves of garlic, minced
- ½ cup coconut milk
- 1 cup mushrooms, sliced
- Pepper and salt to taste
- ½ cup water

Directions:

1. On high fire, heat a saucepan for 2 minutes. Add oil to the pan and swirl to coat bottom and sides. Heat oil for a minute.
2. Add chicken and sear for 4 minutes per side. Transfer chicken to a chopping board and chop into bite-sized chunks.
3. In the same pan, lower fire to medium and sauté garlic for a minute. Add onion and sauté for 3 minutes. Stir in mushrooms and water. Deglaze pot.
4. Return chicken to the pot and mix well. Season with pepper and salt.
5. Cover and lower fire to simmer and cook for 15 minutes.

Nutrition Info:

- Info Per Servings 3.5g Carbs, 62.2g Protein, 11.9g Fat, 383 Calories

Chicken Garam Masala

Servings: 4

Cooking Time: 45 Minutes

Ingredients:

- 1 lb chicken breasts, sliced lengthwise
- 2 tbsp butter
- 1 tbsp olive oil
- 1 yellow bell pepper, finely chopped
- 1 ¼ cups heavy whipping cream
- 1 tbsp fresh cilantro, finely chopped
- Salt and pepper, to taste
- For the garam masala
- 1 tsp ground cumin
- 2 tsp ground coriander
- 1 tsp ground cardamom
- 1 tsp turmeric
- 1 tsp ginger
- 1 tsp paprika
- 1 tsp cayenne, ground
- 1 pinch ground nutmeg

Directions:

1. Set your oven to 400ºF. In a bowl, mix the garam masala spices. Coat the chicken with half of the masala mixture. Heat the olive oil and butter in a frying pan over medium-high heat, and brown the chicken for 3-5 minutes per side. Transfer to a baking dish.

2. To the remaining masala, add heavy cream and bell pepper. Season with salt and pepper and pour over the chicken. Bake in the oven for 20 minutes until the mixture starts to bubble. Garnish with chopped cilantro to serve.

Nutrition Info:

- Info Per Servings 5g Carbs, 33g Protein, 50g Fat, 564 Calories

Lemon Threaded Chicken Skewers

Servings: 4

Cooking Time: 2 Hours 17 Minutes

Ingredients:

- 3 chicken breasts, cut into cubes
- 2 tbsp olive oil, divided
- 2/3 jar preserved lemon, flesh removed, drained
- 2 cloves garlic, minced
- ½ cup lemon juice
- Salt and black pepper to taste
- 1 tsp rosemary leaves to garnish
- 2 to 4 lemon wedges to garnish

Directions:

1. First, thread the chicken onto skewers and set aside.

2. In a wide bowl, mix half of the oil, garlic, salt, pepper, and lemon juice, and add the chicken skewers, and lemon rind. Cover the bowl and let the chicken marinate for at least 2 hours in the refrigerator.

3. When the marinating time is almost over, preheat a grill to 350ºF, and remove the chicken onto the grill. Cook for 6 minutes on each side.

4. Remove and serve warm garnished with rosemary leaves and lemons wedges.

Nutrition Info:

- Info Per Servings 3.5g Carbs, 34g Protein, 11g Fat, 350 Calories

Chili Lime Chicken

Servings: 5
Cooking Time: 30 Minutes
Ingredients:

- 1 lb. chicken breasts, skin and bones removed
- Juice from 1 ½ limes, freshly squeezed
- 1 tbsp. chili powder
- 1 tsp. cumin
- 6 cloves garlic, minced
- Pepper and salt to taste
- 1 cup water
- 4 tablespoon olive oil

Directions:

1. Place all ingredients in a heavy-bottomed pot and give a good stir.
2. Place on high fire and bring it to a boil. Cover, lower fire to a simmer, and cook for 20 minutes.
3. Remove chicken and place in a bowl. Shred using two forks. Return shredded chicken to the pot.
4. Boil for 10 minutes or until sauce is rendered.
5. Serve and enjoy.

Nutrition Info:

- Info Per Servings 1.5g Carbs, 19.3g Protein, 19.5g Fat, 265 Calories

Roasted Chicken With Herbs

Servings: 12
Cooking Time: 50 Minutes
Ingredients:

- 1 whole chicken
- ½ tsp onion powder
- ½ tsp garlic powder
- Salt and black pepper, to taste
- 2 tbsp olive oil
- 1 tsp dry thyme
- 1 tsp dry rosemary
- 1 ½ cups chicken broth
- 2 tsp guar gum

Directions:

1. Rub the chicken with half of the oil, salt, rosemary, thyme, pepper, garlic powder, and onion powder. Place the rest of the oil into a baking dish, and add chicken. Place in the stock, and bake for 40 minutes. Remove the chicken to a platter, and set aside. Stir in the guar gum in a pan over medium heat, and cook until thickening. Place sauce over chicken to serve.

Nutrition Info:

- Info Per Servings 1.1g Carbs, 33g Protein, 15g Fat, 367 Calories

Pork, Beef & Lamb Recipes

Garlic Pork Chops With Mint Pesto

Servings: 4
Cooking Time: 3 Hours 10 Minutes
Ingredients:

- 1 cup parsley
- 1 cup mint
- 1½ onions, chopped
- ⅓ cup pistachios
- 1 tsp lemon zest
- 5 tbsp avocado oil
- Salt, to taste
- 4 pork chops
- 5 garlic cloves, minced
- Juice from 1 lemon

Directions:

1. In a food processor, combine the parsley with avocado oil, mint, pistachios, salt, lemon zest, and 1 onion. Rub the pork with this mixture, place in a bowl, and refrigerate for 1 hour while covered.
2. Remove the chops and set to a baking dish, place in ½ onion, and garlic; sprinkle with lemon juice, and bake for 2 hours in the oven at 250ºF. Split amongst plates and enjoy.

Nutrition Info:

- Info Per Servings 5.5g Carbs, 37g Protein, 40g Fat, 567 Calories

Mushroom Beef Stew

Servings: 5
Cooking Time: 1h 30mins
Ingredients:

- 2 pounds beef chuck roast, cut into 1/2-inch thick strips
- 1/2 medium onion, sliced or diced
- 8 ounces sliced mushrooms
- 2 cups beef broth, divided
- Salt and pepper to taste
- 1 tablespoon butter
- 2 cloves garlic, minced
- 1 tablespoon fresh chopped chives
- 1 tablespoon olive oil

Directions:

1. Heat olive oil in a large skillet over high heat. Stir in beef with salt and pepper; cook, stirring constantly, for 6-7 minutes. Remove beef from the pan and set aside.
2. Add butter, mushrooms and onions into the pan; cook and stir over medium heat.
3. Add garlic and stir for 30 seconds. Stir in 1 cup. broth and simmer 3-4 minutes.
4. Return beef to the pan. Stir in remaining broth and chives; bring to a simmer and cook on low heat for about 1 hour, covered, stirring every 20 minutes.
5. Season with salt and pepper to taste. Serve.

Nutrition Info:

- Info Per Servings 4.1g Carbs, 15.8g Protein, 24.5g Fat, 307 Calories

Baked Pork Meatballs In Pasta Sauce

Servings: 6
Cooking Time: 45 Minutes

Ingredients:

- 2 lb ground pork
- 1 tbsp olive oil
- 1 cup pork rinds, crushed
- 3 cloves garlic, minced
- ½ cup coconut milk
- 2 eggs, beaten
- ½ cup grated Parmesan cheese
- ½ cup grated asiago cheese
- Salt and black pepper to taste
- ¼ cup chopped parsley
- 2 jars sugar-free marinara sauce
- ½ tsp Italian seasoning
- 1 cup Italian blend kinds of cheeses
- Chopped basil to garnish
- Cooking spray

Directions:

1. Preheat the oven to 400ºF, line a cast iron pan with foil and oil it with cooking spray. Set aside.
2. Combine the coconut milk and pork rinds in a bowl. Mix in the ground pork, garlic, Asiago cheese, Parmesan cheese, eggs, salt, and pepper, just until combined. Form balls of the mixture and place them in the prepared pan. Bake in the oven for 20 minutes at a reduced temperature of 370ºF.
3. Transfer the meatballs to a plate. Remove the foil and pour in half of the marinara sauce. Place the meatballs back in the pan and pour the remaining marinara sauce all over them. Sprinkle all over with the Italian blend cheeses, drizzle the olive oil on them, and then sprinkle with Italian seasoning.
4. Cover the pan with foil and put it back in the oven to bake for 10 minutes. After, remove the foil, and continue cooking for 5 minutes. Once ready, take out the pan and garnish with basil. Serve on a bed of squash spaghetti.

Nutrition Info:

- Info Per Servings 4.1g Carbs, 46.2g Protein, 46.8g Fat, 590 Calories

White Wine Lamb Chops

Servings: 6
Cooking Time: 1 Hour And 25 Minutes

Ingredients:

- 6 lamb chops
- 1 tbsp sage
- 1 tsp thyme
- 1 onion, sliced
- 3 garlic cloves, minced
- 2 tbsp olive oil
- ½ cup white wine
- Salt and black pepper, to taste

Directions:

1. Heat the olive oil in a pan. Add onion and garlic and cook for 3 minutes, until soft. Rub the sage and thyme over the lamb chops. Cook the lamb for about 3 minutes per side. Set aside.
2. Pour the white wine and 1 cup of water into the pan, bring the mixture to a boil. Cook until the liquid is reduced by half. Add the chops in the pan, reduce the heat, and let simmer for 1 hour.

Nutrition Info:

- Info Per Servings 4.3g Carbs, 16g Protein, 30g Fat, 397 Calories

Keto Beefy Burritos

Servings: 6
Cooking Time: 25 Minutes
Ingredients:

- 1-pound lean ground beef
- 6 large kale leaves
- 1/4 cup onion
- 1/4 cup low-sodium tomato puree
- 1/4 teaspoon ground cumin
- What you'll need from the store cupboard:
- 1/4 teaspoon black pepper
- ½ tsp salt

Directions:

1. In a medium skillet, brown ground beef for 15 minutes; drain oil on paper towels.
2. Spray skillet with non-stick cooking spray; add onion to cook for 3-5 minutes, until vegetables are softened.
3. Add beef, tomato puree, black pepper, and cumin to onion/pepper mixture.
4. Mix well and cook for 3 to 5 minutes on low heat.
5. Divide the beef mixture among kale leaves.
6. Roll the kale leaves over burrito style, making sure that both ends are folded first, so the mixture does not fall out. Secure with a toothpick.

Nutrition Info:

- Info Per Servings 6.0g Carbs, 25.0g Protein, 32.0g Fat, 412 Calories

Jamaican Pork Oven Roast

Servings: 12
Cooking Time: 4 Hours And 20 Minutes
Ingredients:

- 4 pounds pork roast
- 1 tbsp olive oil
- ¼ cup jerk spice blend
- ½ cup vegetable stock
- Salt and ground pepper, to taste

Directions:

1. Rub the pork with olive oil and the spice blend. Heat a dutch oven over medium heat and sear the meat well on all sides; add in the stock. Cover the pot, reduce the heat, and let cook for 4 hours.

Nutrition Info:

- Info Per Servings 0g Carbs, 23g Protein, 24g Fat, 282 Calories

Classic Meatloaf

Servings: 3
Cooking Time: 40 Mins
Directions:

1. Preheat the oven to 325 degrees F.
2. Place the celery, onion and garlic in a food processor.
3. Place the minced vegetables into a large mixing bowl, and mix in ground chuck, Italian herbs, salt, black pepper, and cayenne pepper.
4. Whisk in the almond flour, stirring well, about 1 minute.
5. Sprinkle the olive oil into a baking dish and place meat into the dish. Shape the ball into a loaf. Bake in the preheated oven for 15 minutes.
6. In a small bowl, mix together ketchup, Dijon mustard, and hot sauce, stirring well to combined.
7. Bake the meatloaf for 30 to 40 more minutes at least 160 degrees F.

Nutrition Info:

- Info Per Servings 10.8g Carbs, 21.6g Protein, 19g Fat, 300 Calories

Garlicky Pork With Bell Peppers

Servings: 4

Cooking Time: 40 Minutes

Ingredients:

- 3 tbsp butter
- 4 pork steaks, bone-in
- 1 cup chicken stock
- Salt and ground black pepper, to taste
- A pinch of lemon pepper
- 3 tbsp olive oil
- 6 garlic cloves, minced
- 2 tbsp fresh parsley, chopped
- 4 bell peppers, sliced
- 1 lemon, sliced

Directions:

1. Heat a pan with 2 tablespoons oil and 2 tablespoons butter over medium-high heat. Add in the pork steaks, season with pepper and salt, cook until browned; remove to a plate. In the same pan, warm the rest of the oil and butter, add garlic and bell pepper and cook for 4 minutes.

2. Pour the chicken stock, lemon slices, salt, lemon pepper, and black pepper, and cook everything for 5 minutes. Return the pork steaks to the pan and cook for 10 minutes. Split the sauce and steaks among plates and enjoy.

Nutrition Info:

- Info Per Servings 6g Carbs, 40g Protein, 25g Fat, 456 Calories

Spicy Pork Stew With Spinach

Servings: 4

Cooking Time: 40 Minutes

Ingredients:

- 1 lb. pork butt, cut into chunks
- 1 onion, chopped
- 4 cloves of garlic, minced
- 1 cup coconut milk, freshly squeezed
- 1 cup spinach leaves, washed and rinsed
- Salt and pepper to taste
- 1 cup water

Directions:

1. In a heavy-bottomed pot, add all ingredients, except for coconut milk and spinach. Mix well.
2. Cover and cook on medium-high fire until boiling. Lower fire to a simmer and cook for 30 minutes undisturbed.
3. Add remaining ingredients and cook on high fire uncovered for 5 minutes. Adjust seasoning if needed.
4. Serve and enjoy.

Nutrition Info:

- Info Per Servings 7.2g Carbs, 30.5g Protein, 34.4g Fat, 458 Calories

Beef Sausage Casserole

Servings: 8
Cooking Time: 60 Minutes

Ingredients:

- ⅓ cup almond flour
- 2 eggs
- 2 pounds beef sausage, chopped
- Salt and black pepper, to taste
- 1 tbsp dried parsley
- ¼ tsp red pepper flakes
- ¼ cup Parmesan cheese, grated
- ¼ tsp onion powder
- ½ tsp garlic powder
- ¼ tsp dried oregano
- 1 cup ricotta cheese
- 1 cup sugar-free marinara sauce
- 1½ cups cheddar cheese, shredded

Directions:

1. Using a bowl, combine the sausage, pepper, pepper flakes, oregano, eggs, Parmesan cheese, onion powder, almond flour, salt, parsley, and garlic powder. Form balls, lay them on a lined baking sheet, place in the oven at 370ºF, and bake for 15 minutes.

2. Remove the balls from the oven and cover with half of the marinara sauce. Pour ricotta cheese all over followed by the rest of the marinara sauce. Scatter the cheddar cheese and bake in the oven for 10 minutes. Allow the meatballs casserole to cool before serving.

Nutrition Info:

- Info Per Servings 4g Carbs, 32g Protein, 35g Fat, 456 Calories

Grilled Flank Steak With Lime Vinaigrette

Servings: 6
Cooking Time: 10 Minutes

Ingredients:

- 2 tablespoons lime juice, freshly squeezed
- ¼ cup chopped fresh cilantro
- 1 tablespoon ground cumin
- ¼ teaspoon red pepper flakes
- ¾ pound flank steak
- 2 tablespoons extra virgin olive oil
- ½ teaspoon ground black pepper
- ¼ tsp salt

Directions:

1. Heat the grill to low, medium heat
2. In a food processor, place all ingredients except for the cumin, red pepper flakes, and flank steak. Pulse until smooth. This will be the vinaigrette sauce. Set aside.
3. Season the flank steak with ground cumin and red pepper flakes and allow to marinate for at least 10 minutes.
4. Place the steak on the grill rack and cook for 5 minutes on each side. Cut into the center to check the doneness of the meat. You can also insert a meat thermometer to check the internal temperature.
5. Remove from the grill and allow to stand for 5 minutes.
6. Slice the steak to 2 inches long and toss the vinaigrette to flavor the meat.
7. Serve with salad if desired.

Nutrition Info:

- Info Per Servings 1.0g Carbs, 13.0g Protein, 1.0g Fat, 65 Calories

Moroccan Beef Stew

Servings: 4

Cooking Time: 40 Minutes

Ingredients:

- 1 medium onion, chopped coarsely
- 2-lbs London broil roast, chopped into 2-inch cubes
- ¼ cup prunes
- 1 ¼ teaspoons curry powder
- ½ teaspoon ground cinnamon
- ½ teaspoon salt
- 2 cups water

Directions:

1. Add all ingredients in a pot on high fire and bring to a boil.
2. Once boiling, lower fire to a simmer and cook for 35 minutes.
3. Adjust seasoning to taste.
4. Serve and enjoy.

Nutrition Info:

- Info Per Servings 8.3g Carbs, 40.6g Protein, 49.6g Fat, 658 Calories

Pork Chops And Peppers

Servings: 4

Cooking Time: 20 Minutes

Ingredients:

- 4 thick pork chops
- 1 onion, chopped
- 2 cloves of garlic, minced
- 2 red and yellow bell peppers, seeded and julienned
- Salt and pepper to taste
- 5 tablespoons oil

Directions:

1. In a large saucepan, place on medium fire and heat 1 tsp oil for 3 minutes.
2. Add pork chop and cook for 5 minutes per side. Season pork chops with salt and pepper.
3. Transfer pork chops to a plate and let it rest.
4. In the same pan, add remaining oil. Increase fire to medium-high and sauté garlic. Stir in onions and bell peppers. Sauté until tender and crisp around 5 minutes.
5. Serve pork chops topped with bell pepper mixture.

Nutrition Info:

- Info Per Servings 4.3g Carbs, 23.9g Protein, 16.3g Fat, 245 Calories

Easy Thai 5-spice Pork Stew

Servings: 9

Cooking Time: 40 Minutes

Ingredients:

- 2 lb. pork butt, cut into chunks
- 2 tbsp. 5-spice powder
- 2 cups coconut milk, freshly squeezed
- 1 ½ tbsp sliced ginger
- 1 cup chopped cilantro
- 1 tsp oil
- Salt and pepper to taste
- ½ cup water

Directions:

1. Place a heavy-bottomed pot on medium-high fire and heat for 2 minutes. Add oil and heat for a minute.
2. Stir in pork chunks and cook for 3 minutes per side.
3. Add ginger, cilantro, pepper, and salt. Sauté for 2 minutes.
4. Add water and deglaze the pot. Stir in 5-spice powder.
5. Cover and simmer for 20 minutes.
6. Stir in coconut milk. Cover and cook for another 10 minutes.
7. Adjust seasoning if needed.
8. Serve and enjoy.

Nutrition Info:

- Info Per Servings 4.4g Carbs, 39.8g Protein, 30.5g Fat, 398 Calories

Bacon Stew With Cauliflower

Servings: 6

Cooking Time: 40 Minutes

Ingredients:

- 8 ounces mozzarella cheese, grated
- 2 cups chicken broth
- ½ tsp garlic powder
- ½ tsp onion powder
- Salt and black pepper, to taste
- 4 garlic cloves, minced
- ¼ cup heavy cream
- 3 cups bacon, chopped
- 1 head cauliflower, cut into florets

Directions:

1. In a pot, combine the bacon with broth, cauliflower, salt, heavy cream, pepper, garlic powder, cheese, onion powder, and garlic, and cook for 35 minutes, share into serving plates, and enjoy.

Nutrition Info:

- Info Per Servings 6g Carbs, 33g Protein, 25g Fat, 380 Calories

Beefy Bbq Ranch

Servings: 4

Cooking Time: 40 Minutes

Ingredients:

- 2-lbs London broil roast, sliced into 2-inch cubes
- 1 Hidden Valley Ranch seasoning mix packet
- 1-pound bacon
- 1 tablespoon barbecue powder
- 1 cup water
- Pepper and salt to taste

Directions:

1. Add all ingredients in a pot on high fire and bring to a boil.
2. Once boiling, lower fire to a simmer and cook for 35 minutes.
3. Adjust seasoning to taste.
4. Serve and enjoy.

Nutrition Info:

- Info Per Servings 8.4g Carbs, 65.3g Protein, 39.7g Fat, 642 Calories

Herby Beef & Veggie Stew

Servings: 4
Cooking Time: 30 Minutes
Ingredients:

- 1 pound ground beef
- 2 tbsp olive oil
- 1 onion, chopped
- 2 garlic cloves, minced
- 14 ounces canned diced tomatoes
- 1 tbsp dried rosemary
- 1 tbsp dried sage
- 1 tbsp dried oregano
- 1 tbsp dried basil
- 1 tbsp dried marjoram
- Salt and black pepper, to taste
- 2 carrots, sliced
- 2 celery stalks, chopped
- 1 cup vegetable broth

Directions:

1. Set a pan over medium heat, add in the olive oil, onion, celery, and garlic, and sauté for 5 minutes. Place in the beef, and cook for 6 minutes. Stir in the tomatoes, carrots, broth, black pepper, oregano, marjoram, basil, rosemary, salt, and sage, and simmer for 15 minutes. Serve and enjoy!

Nutrition Info:

- Info Per Servings 5.2g Carbs, 30g Protein, 13g Fat, 253 Calories

Mustard-lemon Beef

Servings: 4
Cooking Time: 25 Minutes
Ingredients:

- 2 tbsp olive oil
- 1 tbsp fresh rosemary, chopped
- 2 garlic cloves, minced
- 1½ pounds beef rump steak, thinly sliced
- Salt and black pepper, to taste
- 1 shallot, chopped
- ½ cup heavy cream
- ½ cup beef stock
- 1 tbsp mustard
- 2 tsp Worcestershire sauce
- 2 tsp lemon juice
- 1 tsp erythritol
- 2 tbsp butter
- A sprig of rosemary
- A sprig of thyme

Directions:

1. Using a bowl, combine 1 tbsp of oil with pepper, garlic, rosemary, and salt. Toss in the beef to coat, and set aside for some minutes. Heat a pan with the rest of the oil over medium-high heat, place in the beef steak, cook for 6 minutes, flipping halfway through; set aside and keep warm.

2. Set the pan to medium heat, stir in the shallot, and cook for 3 minutes; stir in the stock, Worcestershire sauce, erythritol, thyme, cream, mustard, and rosemary, and cook for 8 minutes.

3. Stir in the butter, lemon juice, pepper, and salt. Get rid of the rosemary and thyme, and remove from heat. Arrange the beef slices on serving plates, sprinkle over the sauce, and enjoy.

Nutrition Info:

- Info Per Servings 5g Carbs, 32g Protein, 30g Fat, 435 Calories

Beef Stuffed Roasted Squash

Servings: 4

Cooking Time: 1 Hour 15 Minutes

Ingredients:

- 2 lb butternut squash, pricked with a fork
- Salt and ground black pepper, to taste
- 3 garlic cloves, minced
- 1 onion, peeled and chopped
- 1 button mushroom, sliced
- 28 ounces canned diced tomatoes
- 1 tsp dried oregano
- ¼ tsp cayenne pepper
- ½ tsp dried thyme
- 1 pound ground beef
- 1 green bell pepper, chopped

Directions:

1. Lay the butternut squash on a lined baking sheet, set in the oven at 400ºF, and bake for 40 minutes. Cut in half, set aside to let cool, deseed, scoop out most of the flesh and let sit. Heat a greased pan over medium-high heat, add in the garlic, mushrooms, onion, and beef, and cook until the meat browns.

2. Stir in the green pepper, salt, thyme, tomatoes, oregano, black pepper, and cayenne, and cook for 10 minutes; stir in the flesh. Stuff the squash halves with the beef mixture, and bake in the oven for 10 minutes. Split into plates and enjoy.

Nutrition Info:

- Info Per Servings 12.4g Carbs, 34g Protein, 14.7g Fat, 406 Calories

Pizzaiola Steak Stew

Servings: 4

Cooking Time: 40 Minutes

Ingredients:

- ¼ cup water
- 2-pounds London broil
- 1 medium sliced onion
- 1 yellow sweet sliced bell pepper
- Half a jar of pasta sauce
- Pepper and salt to taste

Directions:

1. Add all ingredients in a pot on high fire and bring to a boil.
2. Once boiling, lower fire to a simmer and cook for 35 minutes.
3. Adjust seasoning to taste.
4. Serve and enjoy.

Nutrition Info:

- Info Per Servings 5.9g Carbs, 70.7g Protein, 20.6g Fat, 488 Calories

Chili Cheese Taco Dip

Servings: 8
Cooking Time: 25 Minutes
Ingredients:

- 1-pound ground beef
- 1-pound mild Mexican cheese, grated
- 1 can tomato salsa
- 1 packet Mexican spice blend
- 5 tablespoons olive oil
- Salt and pepper to taste
- ½ cup water

Directions:

1. Heat a nonstick saucepan over medium heat for 3 minutes. Heat the oil.
2. Sauté the ground beef until lightly golden, around 8 minutes. Season with pepper, Mexican spice blend, and salt.
3. Add remaining ingredients and give a good stir.
4. Bring to a boil, lower fire to a simmer, and simmer for 10 minutes.

Nutrition Info:

- Info Per Servings 3.1g Carbs, 24.8g Protein, 30.9g Fat, 405 Calories

Caribbean Beef

Servings: 8
Cooking Time: 1 Hour 10 Minutes
Ingredients:

- 2 onions, chopped
- 2 tbsp avocado oil
- 2 pounds beef stew meat, cubed
- 2 red bell peppers, seeded and chopped
- 1 habanero pepper, chopped
- 4 green chilies, chopped
- 14.5 ounces canned diced tomatoes
- 2 tbsp fresh cilantro, chopped
- 4 garlic cloves, minced
- ½ cup vegetable broth
- Salt and black pepper, to taste
- 1 ½ tsp cumin
- ½ cup black olives, chopped
- 1 tsp dried oregano

Directions:

1. Set a pan over medium-high heat and warm avocado oil. Brown the beef on all sides; remove and set aside. Stir-fry in the red bell peppers, green chilies, oregano, garlic, habanero pepper, onions, and cumin, for about 5-6 minutes. Pour in the tomatoes and broth, and cook for 1 hour. Stir in the olives, adjust the seasonings and serve in bowls sprinkled with fresh cilantro.

Nutrition Info:

- Info Per Servings 8g Carbs, 25g Protein, 14g Fat, 305 Calories

Soups, Stew & Salads Recipes

Caesar Salad With Smoked Salmon And Poached Eggs

Servings: 4

Cooking Time: 15 Minutes

Ingredients:

- 3 cups water
- 8 eggs
- 2 cups torn romaine lettuce
- ½ cup smoked salmon, chopped
- 6 slices bacon
- 2 tbsp Heinz low carb Caesar dressing

Directions:

1. Boil the water in a pot over medium heat for 5 minutes and bring to simmer. Crack each egg into a small bowl and gently slide into the water. Poach for 2 to 3 minutes, remove with a perforated spoon, transfer to a paper towel to dry, and plate. Poach the remaining 7 eggs.

2. Put the bacon in a skillet and fry over medium heat until browned and crispy, about 6 minutes, turning once. Remove, allow cooling, and chop in small pieces.

3. Toss the lettuce, smoked salmon, bacon, and caesar dressing in a salad bowl. Divide the salad into 4 plates, top with two eggs each, and serve immediately or chilled.

Nutrition Info:

- Info Per Servings 5g Carbs, 8g Protein, 21g Fat, 260 Calories

Spinach Fruit Salad With Seeds

Servings: 4

Cooking Time: 1 Hour 10 Minutes

Ingredients:

- 2 tablespoons sesame seeds
- 1 tablespoon poppy seeds
- 1 tablespoon minced onion
- 10 ounces fresh spinach - rinsed, dried and torn into bite-size pieces
- 1 quart strawberries - cleaned, hulled and sliced
- 1/2 cup stevia
- 1/2 cup olive oil
- 1/4 cup distilled white vinegar
- 1/4 teaspoon Worcestershire sauce
- 1/4 teaspoon paprika

Directions:

1. Mix together the spinach and strawberry in a large bowl, stir in the sesame seeds, poppy seeds, stevia, olive oil, vinegar, paprika, Worcestershire sauce and onion in a medium bowl. Cover and cool for 1 hour.

2. Pour dressing over salad to combine well. Serve immediately or refrigerate for 15 minutes.

Nutrition Info:

- Info Per Servings 8.6g Carbs, 6g Protein, 18g Fat, 220 Calories

Traditional Greek Salad

Servings: 4
Cooking Time: 10 Minutes
Ingredients:

- 5 tomatoes, chopped
- 1 large cucumber, chopped
- 1 green bell pepper, chopped
- 1 small red onion, chopped
- 16 kalamata olives, chopped
- 4 tbsp capers
- 1 cup feta cheese, chopped
- 1 tsp oregano, dried
- 4 tbsp olive oil
- Salt to taste

Directions:

1. Place tomatoes, bell pepper, cucumber, onion, feta cheese and olives in a bowl; mix to combine well. Season with salt. Combine capers, olive oil, and oregano, in a small bowl. Drizzle with the dressing to serve.

Nutrition Info:

- Info Per Servings 8g Carbs, 9.3g Protein, 28g Fat, 323 Calories

Watermelon And Cucumber Salad

Servings: 10
Cooking Time: 0 Minutes
Ingredients:

- ½ large watermelon, diced
- 1 cucumber, peeled and diced
- 1 red onion, chopped
- ¼ cup feta cheese
- ½ cup heavy cream
- Salt to taste
- 5 tbsp MCT or coconut oil

Directions:

1. Place all ingredients in a bowl.
2. Toss everything to coat.
3. Place in the fridge to cool before serving.

Nutrition Info:

- Info Per Servings 2.5g Carbs, 0.9g Protein, 100g Fat, 910 Calories

Pesto Arugula Salad

Servings: 4

Cooking Time: 10 Minutes

Ingredients:

- ¾ cup red peppers, seeded and chopped
- ¾ cup commercial basil pesto
- 1 small mozzarella cheese ball, diced
- 3 handfuls of arugulas, washed
- Salt and pepper to taste
- 5 tablespoons olive oil

Directions:

1. Mix all ingredients in a salad bowl and toss to coat.
2. Season with salt and pepper to taste.

Nutrition Info:

- Info Per Servings 2.8g Carbs, 6.7g Protein, 20g Fat, 214 Calories

Fruit Salad With Poppy Seeds

Servings: 5

Cooking Time: 25 Mins

Ingredients:

- 1 tablespoon poppy seeds
- 1 head romaine lettuce, torn into bite-size pieces
- 4 ounces shredded Swiss cheese
- 1 avocado- peeled, cored and diced
- 2 teaspoons diced onion
- 1/2 cup lemon juice
- 1/2 cup stevia
- 1/2 teaspoon salt
- 2/3 cup olive oil
- 1 teaspoon Dijon style prepared mustard

Directions:

1. Combine stevia, lemon juice, onion, mustard, and salt in a blender. Process until well blended.
2. Add oil until mixture is thick and smooth. Add poppy seeds, stir just a few seconds or more to mix.
3. In a large serving bowl, toss together the remaining ingredients.
4. Pour dressing over salad just before serving, and toss to coat.

Nutrition Info:

- Info Per Servings 6g Carbs, 4.9g Protein, 20.6g Fat, 277 Calories

Corn And Bacon Chowder

Servings: 8

Cooking Time: 23 Minutes

Ingredients:

- ½ cup bacon, fried and crumbled
- 1 package celery, onion, and bell pepper mix
- 2 cups full-fat milk
- ½ cup sharp cheddar cheese, grated
- 5 tablespoons butter
- Pepper and salt to taste
- 1 cup water

Directions:

1. In a heavy-bottomed pot, melt butter.
2. Saute the bacon and celery for 3 minutes.
3. Turn fire on to medium. Add remaining ingredients and cook for 20 minutes until thick.
4. Serve and enjoy with a sprinkle of crumbled bacon.

Nutrition Info:

- Info Per Servings 4.4g Carbs, 16.6g Protein, 13.6g Fat, 210.5 Calories

Celery Salad

Servings: 4

Cooking Time: 0 Minutes

Ingredients:

- 3 cups celery, thinly sliced
- ½ cup parmigiana cheese, shaved
- 1/3 cup toasted walnuts
- 4 tablespoons extra virgin olive oil
- 1 tablespoon red wine vinegar
- Salt and pepper to taste

Directions:

1. Place the celery, cheese, and walnuts in a bowl.
2. In a smaller bowl, combine the olive oil and vinegar. Season with salt and pepper to taste. Whisk to combine everything.
3. Drizzle over the celery, cheese, and walnuts. Toss to coat.

Nutrition Info:

- Info Per Servings 3.6g Carbs, 4.3g Protein, 14g Fat, 156 Calories

Lobster Salad With Mayo Dressing

Servings: 4

Cooking Time: 1 Hour 10 Minutes

Ingredients:

- 1 small head cauliflower, cut into florets
- ⅓ cup diced celery
- ½ cup sliced black olives
- 2 cups cooked large shrimp
- 1 tbsp dill, chopped
- Dressing:
- ½ cup mayonnaise
- 1 tsp apple cider vinegar
- ¼ tsp celery seeds
- A pinch of black pepper
- 2 tbsp lemon juice
- 2 tsp swerve
- Salt to taste

Directions:

1. Combine the cauliflower, celery, shrimp, and dill in a large bowl. Whisk together the mayonnaise, vinegar, celery seeds, black pepper, sweetener, and lemon juice in another bowl. Season with salt to taste.
2. Pour the dressing over and gently toss to combine; refrigerate for 1 hour. Top with olives to serve.

Nutrition Info:

- Info Per Servings 2g Carbs, 12g Protein, 15g Fat, 182 Calories

Balsamic Cucumber Salad

Servings: 6

Cooking Time: 0 Minutes

Ingredients:

- 1 large English cucumber, halved and sliced
- 1 cup grape tomatoes, halved
- 1 medium red onion, sliced thinly
- ¼ cup balsamic vinaigrette
- ¾ cup feta cheese
- Salt and pepper to taste
- ¼ cup olive oil

Directions:

1. Place all ingredients in a bowl.
2. Toss to coat everything with the dressing.
3. Allow chilling before serving.

Nutrition Info:

- Info Per Servings 9g Carbs, 4.8g Protein, 16.7g Fat, 253 Calories

Beef Reuben Soup

Servings: 6
Cooking Time: 20 Minutes
Ingredients:

- 1 onion, diced
- 6 cups beef stock
- 1 tsp caraway seeds
- 2 celery stalks, diced
- 2 garlic cloves, minced
- 2 cups heavy cream
- 1 cup sauerkraut
- 1 pound corned beef, chopped
- 3 tbsp butter
- 1 ½ cup swiss cheese
- Salt and black pepper, to taste

Directions:

1. Melt the butter in a large pot. Add onion and celery, and fry for 3 minutes until tender. Add garlic and cook for another minute.
2. Pour the beef stock over and stir in sauerkraut, salt, caraway seeds, and add a pinch of pepper. Bring to a boil. Reduce the heat to low, and add the corned beef. Cook for about 15 minutes, adjust the seasoning. Stir in heavy cream and cheese and cook for 1 minute.

Nutrition Info:

- Info Per Servings 8g Carbs, 23g Protein, 37g Fat, 450 Calories

Clam Chowder

Servings: 5
Cooking Time: 10 Minutes
Ingredients:

- 1 can condensed cream of celery soup, undiluted
- 2 cups half-and-half cream
- 2 cans minced/chopped clams, drained
- 1/4 teaspoon ground nutmeg
- 5 tablespoons butter
- Pepper to taste

Directions:

1. In a large saucepan, combine all ingredients. Cook and stir over medium heat until heated through.

Nutrition Info:

- Info Per Servings 3.8g Carbs, 10g Protein, 14g Fat, 251 Calories

Mushroom-broccoli Soup

Servings: 4
Cooking Time: 20 Minutes
Ingredients:

- 1 onion, diced
- 3 cloves of garlic, diced
- 2 cups mushrooms, chopped
- 2 heads of broccoli, cut into florets
- 1 cup full-fat milk
- 3 cups water
- Pepper and salt to taste

Directions:

1. Place a heavy-bottomed pot on medium-high fire and heat for 3 minutes.
2. Add onion, garlic, water, and broccoli. Season generously with pepper and salt.
3. Cover and bring to a boil. Once boiling, lower fire to a simmer and let it cook for 7 minutes.
4. With a handheld blender, puree mixture until smooth and creamy.
5. Stir in mushrooms and milk, cover, and simmer for another 8 minutes.
6. Serve and enjoy.

Nutrition Info:

- Info Per Servings 8.5g Carbs, 3.8g Protein, 1.0g Fat, 58.2 Calories

Bacon And Pea Salad

Servings: 6
Cooking Time: 5 Minutes
Ingredients:

- 4 bacon strips
- 2 cups fresh peas
- ½ cup shredded cheddar cheese
- ½ cup ranch salad dressing
- 1/3 cup chopped red onions
- Salt and pepper to taste
- 3 tablespoons olive oil

Directions:

1. Heat skillet over medium flame and fry the bacon until crispy or until the fat has rendered. Transfer into a plate lined with a paper towel and crumble.
2. In a bowl, combine the rest of the ingredients and toss to coat.
3. Add in the bacon bits last.

Nutrition Info:

- Info Per Servings 2.9g Carbs, 3.5g Protein, 20.4g Fat, 205 Calories

Bacon Tomato Salad

Servings: 6
Cooking Time: 0 Minutes
Ingredients:

- 6 ounces iceberg lettuce blend
- 2 cups grape tomatoes, halved
- ¾ cup coleslaw salad dressing
- ¾ cup cheddar cheese, shredded
- 12 bacon strips, cooked and crumbled
- Salt and pepper to taste

Directions:

1. Put the lettuce and tomatoes in a salad bowl.
2. Drizzle with the dressing and sprinkle with cheese. Season with salt and pepper to taste then mix.
3. Garnish with bacon bits on top.

Nutrition Info:

- Info Per Servings 8g Carbs, 10g Protein, 20g Fat, 268 Calories

Green Mackerel Salad

Servings: 2
Cooking Time: 25 Minutes
Ingredients:

- 2 mackerel fillets
- 2 hard-boiled eggs, sliced
- 1 tbsp coconut oil
- 2 cups green beans
- 1 avocado, sliced
- 4 cups mixed salad greens
- 2 tbsp olive oil
- 2 tbsp lemon juice
- 1 tsp Dijon mustard
- Salt and black pepper, to taste

Directions:

1. Fill a saucepan with water and add the green beans and salt. Cook over medium heat for about 3 minutes. Drain and set aside.

2. Melt the coconut oil in a pan over medium heat. Add the mackerel fillets and cook for about 4 minutes per side, or until opaque and crispy. Divide the green beans between two salad bowls. Top with mackerel, egg, and avocado slices.

3. In a bowl, whisk together the lemon juice, olive oil, mustard, salt, and pepper, and drizzle over the salad.

Nutrition Info:

- Info Per Servings 7.6g Carbs, 27.3g Protein, 41.9g Fat, 525 Calories

Chicken And Cauliflower Rice Soup

Servings: 8
Cooking Time: 20 Mins
Ingredients:

- 2 cooked, boneless chicken breast halves, shredded
- 2 packages Steamed Cauliflower Rice
- 1/4 cup celery, chopped
- 1/2 cup onion, chopped
- 4 garlic cloves, minced
- Salt and ground black pepper to taste
- 2 teaspoons poultry seasoning
- 4 cups chicken broth
- ½ cup butter
- 2 cups heavy cream

Directions:

1. Heat butter in a large pot over medium heat, add onion, celery and garlic cloves to cook until tender. Meanwhile, place the riced cauliflower steam bags in the microwave following directions on the package.

2. Add the riced cauliflower, seasoning, salt and black pepper to butter mixture, saute them for 7 minutes on medium heat, stirring constantly to well combined.

3. Bring cooked chicken breast halves, broth and heavy cream to a broil. When it starts boiling, lower the heat, cover and simmer for 15 minutes.

Nutrition Info:

- Info Per Servings 6g Carbs, 27g Protein, 30g Fat, 415 Calories

Garlic Chicken Salad

Servings: 4

Cooking Time: 15 Minutes

Ingredients:

- 2 chicken breasts, boneless, skinless, flattened
- Salt and black pepper to taste
- 2 tbsp garlic powder
- 1 tsp olive oil
- 1 ½ cups mixed salad greens
- 1 tbsp red wine vinegar
- 1 cup crumbled blue cheese

Directions:

1. Season the chicken with salt, black pepper, and garlic powder. Heat oil in a pan over high heat and fry the chicken for 4 minutes on both sides until golden brown. Remove chicken to a cutting board and let cool before slicing.

2. Toss salad greens with red wine vinegar and share the salads into 4 plates. Divide chicken slices on top and sprinkle with blue cheese. Serve salad with carrots fries.

Nutrition Info:

- Info Per Servings 4g Carbs, 14g Protein, 23g Fat, 286 Calories

Homemade Cold Gazpacho Soup

Servings: 6

Cooking Time: 15 Minutes

Ingredients:

- 2 small green peppers, roasted
- 2 large red peppers, roasted
- 2 medium avocados, flesh scoped out
- 2 garlic cloves
- 2 spring onions, chopped
- 1 cucumber, chopped
- 1 cup olive oil
- 2 tbsp lemon juice
- 4 tomatoes, chopped
- 7 ounces goat cheese
- 1 small red onion, chopped
- 2 tbsp apple cider vinegar
- Salt to taste

Directions:

1. Place the peppers, tomatoes, avocados, red onion, garlic, lemon juice, olive oil, vinegar, and salt, in a food processor. Pulse until your desired consistency is reached. Taste and adjust the seasoning.

2. Transfer the mixture to a pot. Stir in cucumber and spring onions. Cover and chill in the fridge at least 2 hours. Divide the soup between 6 bowls. Serve very cold, generously topped with goat cheese and an extra drizzle of olive oil.

Nutrition Info:

- Info Per Servings 6.5g Carbs, 7.5g Protein, 45.8g Fat, 528 Calories

Chicken Stock And Green Bean Soup

Servings: 6
Cooking Time:1h 30 Mins
Ingredients:

- 2 tablespoons butter
- 1/2 onion, diced
- 2 ribs celery, diced
- 1 cup green beans
- 6 bacon slices
- What you'll need from the store cupboard:
- 3 cloves garlic, sliced
- 1 quart chicken stock
- 2 1/2 cups water
- 1 bay leaf
- Salt and ground black pepper to taste

Directions:

1. In a large pot over medium-low heat, melt the butter. Add the onions, celery, and sliced garlic, cook for 5-8 minutes, or until onions are soft.
2. Stir in in bacon slices, bay leaf, and green beans. Add chicken stock and water, stirring until well combined, and simmer for 1 hour and 15 minutes, or green beans are soft. Sprinkle with salt and black pepper before serving.

Nutrition Info:

- Info Per Servings 7g Carbs, 15.1g Protein, 11.3g Fat, 208.6 Calories

Sour Cream And Cucumbers

Servings: 8
Cooking Time: 0 Minutes
Ingredients:

- ½ cup sour cream
- 3 tablespoons white vinegar
- 4 medium cucumbers, sliced thinly
- 1 small sweet onion, sliced thinly
- Salt and pepper to taste
- 3 tablespoons olive oil

Directions:

1. In a bowl, whisk the sour cream and vinegar. Season with salt and pepper to taste. Whisk until well-combined.
2. Add in the cucumber and the rest of the ingredients.
3. Toss to coat.
4. Allow chilling before serving.

Nutrition Info:

- Info Per Servings 4.8g Carbs, 0.9g Protein, 8.3g Fat, 96 Calories

Tuna Salad With Lettuce & Olives

Servings: 2
Cooking Time: 5 Minutes
Ingredients:

- 1 cup canned tuna, drained
- 1 tsp onion flakes
- 3 tbsp mayonnaise
- 1 cup shredded romaine lettuce
- 1 tbsp lime juice
- Sea salt, to taste
- 6 black olives, pitted and sliced

Directions:

1. Combine the tuna, mayonnaise, lime juice, and salt in a small bowl; mix to combine well. In a salad platter, arrange the shredded lettuce and onion flakes. Spread the tuna mixture over; top with black olives to serve.

Nutrition Info:

- Info Per Servings 2g Carbs, 18.5g Protein, 20g Fat, 248 Calories

Sauces And Dressing Recipes

Sriracha Mayo

Servings: 4
Cooking Time: 5 Minutes
Ingredients:

- ½ cup mayonnaise
- 2 tablespoons Sriracha sauce
- ½ teaspoon garlic powder
- ½ teaspoon onion powder
- ¼ teaspoon paprika

Directions:

1. In a small bowl, whisk together the mayonnaise, Sriracha, garlic powder, onion powder, and paprika until well mixed.
2. Pour into an airtight glass container, and keep in the refrigerator for up to 1 week.

Nutrition Info:

- Info Per Servings Calories: 2g Carbs, 1g Protein, 22g Fat, 201 Calories

Alfredo Sauce

Servings: 2
Cooking Time: 10 Minutes
Ingredients:

- 4 tablespoons butter
- 2 ounces cream cheese
- 1 cup heavy (whipping) cream
- ½ cup grated Parmesan cheese
- 1 garlic clove, finely minced
- 1 teaspoon dried Italian seasoning
- Pink Himalayan salt
- Freshly ground black pepper

Directions:

1. In a heavy medium saucepan over medium heat, combine the butter, cream cheese, and heavy cream. Whisk slowly and constantly until the butter and cream cheese melt.
2. Add the Parmesan, garlic, and Italian seasoning. Continue to whisk until everything is well blended. Turn the heat to medium-low and simmer, stirring occasionally, for 5 to 8 minutes to allow the sauce to blend and thicken.
3. Season with pink Himalayan salt and pepper, and stir to combine.
4. Toss with your favorite hot, precooked, keto-friendly noodles and serve.
5. Keep this sauce in a sealed glass container in the refrigerator for up to 4 days.

Nutrition Info:

- Info Per Servings 2g Carbs, 5g Protein, 30g Fat, 294 Calories

Dijon Vinaigrette

Servings: 4
Cooking Time: 5 Minutes
Ingredients:

- 2 tablespoons Dijon mustard
- Juice of ½ lemon
- 1 garlic clove, finely minced
- 1½ tablespoons red wine vinegar
- Pink Himalayan salt
- Freshly ground black pepper
- 3 tablespoons olive oil

Directions:

1. In a small bowl, whisk the mustard, lemon juice, garlic, and red wine vinegar until well combined. Season with pink Himalayan salt and pepper, and whisk again.
2. Slowly add the olive oil, a little bit at a time, whisking constantly.
3. Keep in a sealed glass container in the refrigerator for up to 1 week.

Nutrition Info:

- Info Per Servings 1g Carbs, 1g Protein, 11g Fat, 99 Calories

Greek Yogurt Dressing

Servings: 2
Cooking Time: 0 Minutes
Ingredients:

- ¼ tsp ground ginger
- ½ tsp prepared mustard
- 2 tbsp low-fat mayonnaise
- ½ cup plain Greek yogurt
- Salt and pepper to taste

Directions:

1. In a bowl, whisk well all ingredients.
2. Adjust seasoning to taste.
3. Serve and enjoy with your favorite salad greens.

Nutrition Info:

- Info Per Servings 3.5g Carbs, 3.0g Protein, 2.8g Fat, 51 Calories

Cheesy Avocado Dip

Servings:
Cooking Time: 20 Minutes
Ingredients:

- 1/2 medium ripe avocado, peeled and pitted
- 2 crumbled blue cheese
- 1 freshly squeezed lemon juice
- 1/2 kosher salt
- 1/2 cup water

Directions:

1. Scoop the flesh of the avocado into the bowl of a food processor fitted with the blade attachment or blender.
2. Add the blue cheese, lemon juice, and salt. Blend until smooth and creamy, 30 to 40 seconds.
3. With the motor running, add the water and blend until the sauce is thinned and well-combined.

Nutrition Info:

- Info Per Servings 2.9g Carbs, 3.5g Protein, 7.2g Fat, 86 Calories

Artichoke Pesto Dip

Servings: 1
Cooking Time: 20 Minutes
Ingredients:

- 1 jar marinated artichoke hearts
- 8 ounces cream cheese (at room temperature)
- 4 ounces parmesan cheese (grated)
- 2 tablespoons basil pesto
- ¼ cup shelled pistachio (chopped, optional)

Directions:

1. Preheat oven to 375oF.
2. Drain and chop artichoke hearts.
3. Mix artichokes, cream cheese, parmesan, and pesto.
4. Pour into 4 ramekins evenly.
5. Bake for 15-20 minutes.

Nutrition Info:

- Info Per Servings 5g Carbs, 8g Protein, 19g Fat, 214 Calories

Roasted Garlic Lemon Dip

Servings: 3
Cooking Time: 30 Minutes
Ingredients:

- 3 medium lemons
- 3 cloves garlic, peeled and smashed
- 5 tablespoons olive oil, divided
- 1/2 teaspoon kosher salt
- Pepper to taste
- Salt
- Pepper

Directions:

1. Arrange a rack in the middle of the oven and heat to 400°F.
2. Cut the lemons in half crosswise and remove the seeds. Place the lemons cut-side up in a small baking dish. Add the garlic and drizzle with 2 tablespoons of the oil.
3. Roast until the lemons are tender and lightly browned, about 30 minutes. Remove the baking dish to a wire rack.
4. When the lemons are cool enough to handle, squeeze the juice into the baking dish. Discard the lemon pieces and any remaining seeds. Pour the contents of the baking dish, including the garlic, into a blender or mini food processor. Add the remaining 3 tablespoons oil and salt. Process until the garlic is completely puréed, and the sauce is emulsified and slightly thickened. Serve warm or at room temperature.

Nutrition Info:

- Info Per Servings 4.8g Carbs, 0.6g Protein, 17g Fat, 165 Calories

Keto Ranch Dip

Servings: 8
Cooking Time: 10 Minutes
Ingredients:

- 1 cup egg white, beaten
- 1 lemon juice, freshly squeezed
- Salt and pepper to taste
- 1 teaspoon mustard paste
- 1 cup olive oil
- Salt and pepper to taste

Directions:

1. Add all ingredients to a pot and bring to a simmer. Stir frequently.
2. Simmer for 10 minutes.
3. Adjust seasoning to taste.

Nutrition Info:

- Info Per Servings 1.2g Carbs, 3.4g Protein, 27.1g Fat, 258 Calories

Tzatziki

Servings: 4

Cooking Time: 10 Minutes, Plus At Least 30 Minutes To Chill

Ingredients:

- ½ large English cucumber, unpeeled
- 1½ cups Greek yogurt (I use Fage)
- 2 tablespoons olive oil
- Large pinch pink Himalayan salt
- Large pinch freshly ground black pepper
- Juice of ½ lemon
- 2 garlic cloves, finely minced
- 1 tablespoon fresh dill

Directions:

1. Halve the cucumber lengthwise, and use a spoon to scoop out and discard the seeds.
2. Grate the cucumber with a zester or grater onto a large plate lined with a few layers of paper towels. Close the paper towels around the grated cucumber, and squeeze as much water out of it as you can. (This can take a while and can require multiple paper towels. You can also allow it to drain overnight in a strainer or wrapped in a few layers of cheesecloth in the fridge if you have the time.)
3. In a food processor (or blender), blend the yogurt, olive oil, pink Himalayan salt, pepper, lemon juice, and garlic until fully combined.
4. Transfer the mixture to a medium bowl, and mix in the fresh dill and grated cucumber.
5. I like to chill this sauce for at least 30 minutes before serving. Keep in a sealed glass container in the refrigerator for up to 1 week.

Nutrition Info:

- Info Per Servings 5g Carbs, 8g Protein, 11g Fat, 149 Calories

Green Jalapeno Sauce

Servings: 1

Cooking Time: 0 Minutes

Ingredients:

- ½ avocado
- 1 large jalapeno
- 1 cup fresh cilantro
- 2 tablespoons extra virgin olive oil
- 3 tablespoons water
- Water
- ½ teaspoon salt

Directions:

1. Add all ingredients in a blender.
2. Blend until smooth and creamy.
3. Serve and enjoy.

Nutrition Info:

- Info Per Servings 10g Carbs, 2.4g Protein, 42g Fat, 407 Calories

Peanut Sauce

Servings: 4
Cooking Time: 5 Minutes
Ingredients:

- ½ cup creamy peanut butter (I use Justin's)
- 2 tablespoons soy sauce (or coconut aminos)
- 1 teaspoon Sriracha sauce
- 1 teaspoon toasted sesame oil
- 1 teaspoon garlic powder

Directions:

1. In a food processor (or blender), blend the peanut butter, soy sauce, Sriracha sauce, sesame oil, and garlic powder until thoroughly mixed.
2. Pour into an airtight glass container and keep in the refrigerator for up to 1 week.

Nutrition Info:

- Info Per Servings Calories: 185; Total Fat: 15g; Carbs: 8g; Net Carbs: 6g; Fiber: 2g; Protein: 7g

Avocado Mayo

Servings: 4
Cooking Time: 5 Minutes
Ingredients:

- 1 medium avocado, cut into chunks
- ½ teaspoon ground cayenne pepper
- Juice of ½ lime
- 2 tablespoons fresh cilantro leaves (optional)
- Pinch pink Himalayan salt
- ¼ cup olive oil

Directions:

1. In a food processor (or blender), blend the avocado, cayenne pepper, lime juice, cilantro, and pink Himalayan salt until all the ingredients are well combined and smooth.
2. Slowly incorporate the olive oil, adding 1 tablespoon at a time, pulsing the food processor in between.
3. Keep in a sealed glass container in the refrigerator for up to 1 week.

Nutrition Info:

- Info Per Servings 1g Carbs, 1g Protein, 5g Fat, 58 Calories

Green Goddess Dressing

Servings: 4
Cooking Time: 5 Minutes
Ingredients:

- 2 tablespoon buttermilk
- ¼ cup Greek yogurt
- 1 teaspoon apple cider vinegar
- 1 garlic clove, minced
- 1 tablespoon olive oil
- 1 tablespoon fresh parsley leaves

Directions:

1. In a food processor (or blender), combine the buttermilk, yogurt, apple cider vinegar, garlic, olive oil, and parsley. Blend until fully combined.
2. Pour into a sealed glass container and chill in the refrigerator for at least 30 minutes before serving. This dressing will keep in the fridge for up to 1 week.

Nutrition Info:

- Info Per Servings 1g Carbs, 1g Protein, 6g Fat, 62 Calories

Garlic Aioli

Servings: 4
Cooking Time: 5 Minutes, Plus 30 Minutes To Chill
Ingredients:

- ½ cup mayonnaise
- 2 garlic cloves, minced
- Juice of 1 lemon
- 1 tablespoon chopped fresh flat-leaf Italian parsley
- 1 teaspoon chopped chives
- Pink Himalayan salt
- Freshly ground black pepper

Directions:

1. In a food processor (or blender), combine the mayonnaise, garlic, lemon juice, parsley, and chives, and season with pink Himalayan salt and pepper. Blend until fully combined.
2. Pour into a sealed glass container and chill in the refrigerator for at least 30 minutes before serving. (This sauce will keep in the fridge for up to 1 week.)

Nutrition Info:

- Info Per Servings Calories: 3g Carbs, 1g Protein, 22g Fat, 204 Calories

Keto Thousand Island Dressing

Servings: 10
Cooking Time: 10 Minutes
Ingredients:

- 1 cup mayonnaise
- 1 tablespoon lemon juice, freshly squeezed
- 4 tablespoons dill pickles, chopped
- 1 teaspoon Tabasco
- 1 shallot chopped finely
- Salt and pepper to taste

Directions:

1. Add all ingredients to a pot and bring to a simmer. Stir frequently.
2. Simmer for 10 minutes.
3. Adjust seasoning to taste.

Nutrition Info:

- Info Per Servings 2.3g Carbs, 1.7g Protein, 7.8g Fat, 85 Calories

Caesar Dressing

Servings: 4
Cooking Time: 5 Minutes
Ingredients:

- ½ cup mayonnaise
- 1 tablespoon Dijon mustard
- Juice of ½ lemon
- ½ teaspoon Worcestershire sauce
- Pinch pink Himalayan salt
- Pinch freshly ground black pepper
- ¼ cup grated Parmesan cheese

Directions:

1. In a medium bowl, whisk together the mayonnaise, mustard, lemon juice, Worcestershire sauce, pink Himalayan salt, and pepper until fully combined.
2. Add the Parmesan cheese, and whisk until creamy and well blended.
3. Keep in a sealed glass container in the refrigerator for up to 1 week.

Nutrition Info:

- Info Per Servings Calories: 2g Carbs, 2g Protein, 23g Fat, 222 Calories

Fat-burning Dressing

Servings: 6

Cooking Time: 3 Minutes

Ingredients:

- 2 tablespoons coconut oil
- ¼ cup olive oil
- 2 cloves of garlic, minced
- 2 tablespoons freshly chopped herbs of your choice
- ¼ cup mayonnaise
- Salt and pepper to taste

Directions:

1. Heat the coconut oil and olive oil and sauté the garlic until fragrant in a saucepan.
2. Allow cooling slightly before adding the mayonnaise.
3. Season with salt and pepper to taste.

Nutrition Info:

- Info Per Servings 0.6g Carbs, 14.1g Protein, 22.5g Fat, 262 Calories

Buttery Dijon Sauce

Servings: 2

Cooking Time: 0 Minutes

Ingredients:

- 3 parts brown butter
- 1-part vinegar or citrus juice or a combo
- 1-part strong Dijon mustard
- A small handful of flat-leaf parsley (optional)
- 3/4 teaspoon freshly ground pepper
- 1 teaspoon salt

Directions:

1. Add everything to a food processor and blitz until just smooth.
2. You can also mix this up with an immersion blender. Use immediately or store in the refrigerator for up to one day. Blend again before use.

Nutrition Info:

- Info Per Servings 0.7g Carbs, 0.4g Protein, 34.4g Fat, 306 Calories

Ketogenic-friendly Gravy

Servings: 6

Cooking Time: 10 Minutes

Ingredients:

- 2 tablespoons butter
- 1 white onion, chopped
- ¼ cup coconut milk
- 2 cups bone broth
- 1 tablespoon balsamic vinegar
- Salt and pepper to taste

Directions:

1. Add all ingredients to a pot and bring to a simmer. Stir frequently.
2. Simmer for 10 minutes.
3. Adjust seasoning to taste.

Nutrition Info:

- Info Per Servings 1.1g Carbs, 0.2g Protein, 6.3g Fat, 59 Calories

Lemon Tahini Sauce

Servings: 2

Cooking Time: 5 Minutes

Ingredients:

- 1/2 cup packed fresh herbs, such as parsley, basil, mint, cilantro, dill, or chives
- 1/4 cup tahini
- Juice of 1 lemon
- 1/2 teaspoon kosher salt
- 1 tablespoon water

Directions:

1. Place all the ingredients in the bowl of a food processor fitted with the blade attachment or a blender. Process continuously until the herbs are finely minced, and the sauce is well-blended, 3 to 4 minutes.
2. Serve immediately or store in a covered container in the refrigerator until ready to serve.

Nutrition Info:

- Info Per Servings 4.3g Carbs, 2.8g Protein, 8.1g Fat, 94 Calories

Chunky Blue Cheese Dressing

Servings: 4

Cooking Time: 5 Minutes

Ingredients:

- ½ cup sour cream
- ½ cup mayonnaise
- Juice of ½ lemon
- ½ teaspoon Worcestershire sauce
- Pink Himalayan salt
- Freshly ground black pepper
- 2 ounces crumbled blue cheese

Directions:

1. In a medium bowl, whisk the sour cream, mayonnaise, lemon juice, and Worcestershire sauce. Season with pink Himalayan salt and pepper, and whisk again until fully combined.
2. Fold in the crumbled blue cheese until well combined.
3. Keep in a sealed glass container in the refrigerator for up to 1 week.

Nutrition Info:

- Info Per Servings 3g Carbs, 7g Protein, 32g Fat, 306 Calories

Vegetarian Fish Sauce

Servings: 16

Cooking Time: 20 Minutes

Ingredients:

- 1/4 cup dried shiitake mushrooms
- 1-2 tbsp tamari (for a depth of flavor)
- 3 tbsp coconut aminos
- 1 ¼ cup water
- 2 tsp sea salt

Directions:

1. To a small saucepan, add water, coconut aminos, dried shiitake mushrooms, and sea salt. Bring to a boil, then cover, reduce heat, and simmer for 15-20 minutes.
2. Remove from heat and let cool slightly. Pour liquid through a fine-mesh strainer into a bowl, pressing on the mushroom mixture with a spoon to squeeze out any remaining liquid.
3. To the bowl, add tamari. Taste and adjust as needed, adding more sea salt for saltiness.
4. Store in a sealed container in the refrigerator for up to 1 month and shake well before use. Or pour into an ice cube tray, freeze, and store in a freezer-safe container for up to 2 months.

Nutrition Info:

- Info Per Servings 5g Carbs, 0.3g Protein, 2g Fat, 39.1 Calories

Fish And Seafood Recipes

Chili-garlic Salmon

Servings: 4

Cooking Time: 15 Minutes

Ingredients:

- 5 tbsp. sweet chili sauce
- ¼ cup coconut aminos
- 4 salmon fillets
- 3 tbsp. green onions, chopped
- 3 cloves garlic, peeled and minced
- Pepper to taste

Directions:

1. Place a trivet in a large saucepan and pour a cup or two of water into the pan. Bring to a boil.
2. In a small bowl, whisk well sweet chili sauce, garlic, and coconut aminos.
3. Place salmon in a heatproof dish that fits inside a saucepan. Season salmon with pepper. Drizzle with sweet chili sauce mixture. Sprinkle green onions on top of the filet.
4. Seal dish with foil. Place the dish on the trivet inside the saucepan. Cover and steam for 15 minutes.
5. Serve and enjoy.

Nutrition Info:

- Info Per Servings 0.9g Carbs, 65.4g Protein, 14.4g Fat, 409 Calories

Baked Salmon With Pistachio Crust

Serves:4

Cooking Time：35 Minutes

Ingredients:

- 4 salmon fillets
- ¼ cup mayonnaise
- ½ cup ground pistachios
- 1 chopped shallot
- 2 tsp lemon zest
- 1 tbsp olive oil
- A pinch of pepper
- 1 cup heavy cream

Directions:

1. Preheat oven to 375 °F. Brush salmon with mayo and season with salt and pepper. Coat with pistachios. Place in a lined baking dish and bake for 15 minutes. Heat the olive oil in a saucepan and sauté shallot for 3 minutes. Stir in heavy cream and lemon zest. Bring to a boil and cook until thickened. Serve salmon with the sauce.

Nutrition Info:

- Per Serves 6g Carbs; 34g Protein; 47g Fat ; 563 Calories

Red Curry Halibut

Servings: 4
Cooking Time: 15 Minutes
Ingredients:

- 4 halibut fillets, skin removed
- 1 cup chopped tomatoes
- 3 green curry leaves
- 2 tbsp. chopped cilantro
- 1 tbsp. lime juice, freshly squeezed
- 3 tbsp olive oil
- Pepper and salt to taste

Directions:

1. Place a trivet in a large saucepan and pour a cup or two of water into the pan. Bring to a boil.
2. Place halibut in a heatproof dish that fits inside the saucepan. Season halibut with pepper and salt. Drizzle with olive oil. Sprinkle chopped tomatoes, curry leaves, chopped cilantro, and lime juice.
3. Seal dish with foil. Place the dish on the trivet inside the saucepan. Cover and steam for 15 minutes.
4. Serve and enjoy.

Nutrition Info:

- Info Per Servings 1.8g Carbs, 76.1g Protein, 15.5g Fat, 429 Calories

Tilapia With Olives & Tomato Sauce

Servings: 4
Cooking Time: 30 Minutes
Ingredients:

- 4 tilapia fillets
- 2 garlic cloves, minced
- 2 tsp oregano
- 14 ounces diced tomatoes
- 1 tbsp olive oil
- ½ red onion, chopped
- 2 tbsp parsley
- ¼ cup kalamata olives

Directions:

1. Heat the olive oil in a skillet over medium heat and cook the onion for about 3 minutes. Add garlic and oregano and cook for 30 seconds. Stir in tomatoes and bring the mixture to a boil. Reduce the heat and simmer for 5 minutes. Add olives and tilapia, and cook for about 8 minutes. Serve the tilapia with tomato sauce.

Nutrition Info:

- Info Per Servings 6g Carbs, 23g Protein, 15g Fat, 282 Calories

Red Cabbage Tilapia Taco Bowl

Servings: 4
Cooking Time: 20 Minutes
Ingredients:

- 2 cups cauli rice
- Water for sprinkling
- 2 tsp ghee
- 4 tilapia fillets, cut into cubes
- ¼ tsp taco seasoning
- Pink salt and chili pepper to taste
- ¼ head red cabbage, shredded
- 1 ripe avocado, pitted and chopped

Directions:

1. Sprinkle cauli rice in a bowl with a little water and microwave for 3 minutes. Fluff after with a fork and set aside. Melt ghee in a skillet over medium heat, rub the tilapia with the taco seasoning, salt, and chili pepper, and fry until brown on all sides, for about 8 minutes in total.
2. Transfer to a plate and set aside. In 4 serving bowls, share the cauli rice, cabbage, fish, and avocado. Serve with chipotle lime sour cream dressing.

Nutrition Info:

- Info Per Servings 4g Carbs, 16.5g Protein, 23.4g Fat, 269 Calories

Shrimp In Curry Sauce

Servings: 2

Cooking Time: 25 Minutes

Ingredients:

- ½ ounces grated Parmesan cheese
- 1 tbsp water
- 1 egg, beaten
- ¼ tsp curry powder
- 2 tsp almond flour
- 12 shrimp, shelled
- 3 tbsp coconut oil
- Sauce
- 2 tbsp curry leaves
- 2 tbsp butter
- ½ onion, diced
- ½ cup heavy cream
- ½ ounce cheddar

Directions:

1. Combine all dry ingredients for the batter. Melt the coconut oil in a skillet over medium heat. Dip the shrimp in the egg first, and then coat with the dry mixture. Fry until golden and crispy.

2. In another skillet, melt the butter. Add onion and cook for 3 minutes. Add curry leaves and cook for 30 seconds. Stir in heavy cream and cheddar and cook until thickened. Add the shrimp and coat well. Serve warm.

Nutrition Info:

- Info Per Servings 4.3g Carbs, 24.4g Protein, 41g Fat, 560 Calories

Angel Hair Shirataki With Creamy Shrimp

Serves:4

Cooking Time：25 Minutes

Ingredients:

- 2 (8 oz) packs angel hair shirataki noodles
- 1 tbsp olive oil
- 1 lb shrimp, deveined
- 2 tbsp unsalted butter
- 6 garlic cloves, minced
- ½ cup dry white wine
- 1 ½ cups heavy cream
- ½ cup grated Asiago cheese
- 2 tbsp chopped fresh parsley

Directions:

1. Heat olive oil in a skillet, season the shrimp with salt and pepper, and cook on both sides, 2 minutes; set aside. Melt butter in the skillet and sauté garlic. Stir in wine and cook until reduced by half, scraping the bottom of the pan to deglaze. Stir in heavy cream. Let simmer for 1 minute and stir in Asiago cheese to melt. Return the shrimp to the sauce and sprinkle the parsley on top. Bring 2 cups of water to a boi. Strain shirataki pasta and rinse under hot running water. Allow proper draining and pour the shirataki pasta into the boiling water. Cook for 3 minutes and strain again. Place a dry skillet and stir-fry the pasta until dry, 1-2 minutes. Season with salt and plate. Top with the shrimp sauce and serve.

Nutrition Info:

- Per Serves 6.3g Carbs; 33g Protein ; 32g Fats; 493 Calories

Spicy Sea Bass With Hazelnuts

Servings: 2

Cooking Time: 30 Minutes

Ingredients:

- 2 sea bass fillets
- 2 tbsp butter
- ⅓ cup roasted hazelnuts
- A pinch of cayenne pepper

Directions:

1. Preheat your oven to 425 ℉. Line a baking dish with waxed paper. Melt the butter and brush it over the fish. In a food processor, combine the rest of the ingredients. Coat the sea bass with the hazelnut mixture. Place in the oven and bake for about 15 minutes.

Nutrition Info:

- Info Per Servings 2.8g Carbs, 40g Protein, 31g Fat, 467 Calories

Air Fryer Seasoned Salmon Fillets

Servings: 4

Cooking Time: 10 Mins

Ingredients:

- 2 lbs. salmon fillets
- 1 tsp. stevia
- 2 tbsp. whole grain mustard
- 1 clove of garlic, minced
- 1/2 tsp. thyme leaves
- 2 tsp. extra-virgin olive oil
- Cooking spray
- Salt and black pepper to taste

Directions:

1. Preheat your Air Fryer to 390 degrees F.

2. Season salmon fillets with salt and pepper.

3. Add together the mustard, garlic, stevia, thyme, and oil in a bowl, stir to combined well. Rub the seasoning mixture on top of salmon fillets.

4. Spray the Air Fryer basket with cooking spray and cook seasoned fillets for 10 minutes until crispy. Let it cool before serving.

Nutrition Info:

- Info Per Servings 14g Carbs, 18g Protein, 10g Fat, 238 Calories

Thyme-sesame Crusted Halibut

Servings: 2

Cooking Time: 15 Minutes

Ingredients:

- 8 oz. halibut, cut into 2 portions
- 1 tbsp. lemon juice, freshly squeezed
- 1 tsp. dried thyme leaves
- 1 tbsp. sesame seeds, toasted
- Salt and pepper to taste

Directions:

1. Place a trivet in a large saucepan and pour a cup or two of water into the pan. Bring it to a boil.

2. Place halibut in a heatproof dish that fits inside a saucepan. Season with lemon juice, salt, and pepper. Sprinkle with dried thyme leaves and sesame seeds.

3. Seal dish with foil. Place the dish on the trivet inside the saucepan. Cover and steam for 15 minutes.

4. Serve and enjoy.

Nutrition Info:

- Info Per Servings 4.2g Carbs, 17.5g Protein, 17.7g Fat, 246 Calories

Coconut Milk Sauce Over Crabs

Servings: 6

Cooking Time: 20 Minutes

Ingredients:

* 2-pounds crab quartered
* 1 can coconut milk
* 1 thumb-size ginger, sliced
* 1 onion, chopped
* 3 cloves of garlic, minced
* Pepper and salt to taste

Directions:

1. Place a heavy-bottomed pot on medium-high fire and add all ingredients.
2. Cover and bring to a boil, lower fire to a simmer, and simmer for 20 minutes.
3. Serve and enjoy.

Nutrition Info:

* Info Per Servings 6.3g Carbs, 29.3g Protein, 11.3g Fat, 244.1 Calories

Lemon Garlic Shrimp

Servings: 6

Cooking Time: 22 Minutes

Ingredients:

* ½ cup butter, divided
* 2 lb shrimp, peeled and deveined
* Pink salt and black pepper to taste
* ¼ tsp sweet paprika
* 1 tbsp minced garlic
* 3 tbsp water
* 1 lemon, zested and juiced
* 2 tbsp chopped parsley

Directions:

1. Melt half of the butter in a large skillet over medium heat, season the shrimp with salt, pepper, paprika, and add to the butter. Stir in the garlic and cook the shrimp for 4 minutes on both sides until pink. Remove to a bowl and set aside.

2. Put the remaining butter in the skillet; include the lemon zest, juice, and water. Cook until the butter has melted, about 1 minute. Add the shrimp, parsley, and adjust the taste with salt and black pepper. Cook for 2 minutes on low heat. Serve the shrimp and sauce with squash pasta.

Nutrition Info:

* Info Per Servings 2g Carbs, 13g Protein, 22g Fat, 258 Calories

Grilled Shrimp With Chimichurri Sauce

Servings: 4

Cooking Time: 55 Minutes

Ingredients:

- 1 pound shrimp, peeled and deveined
- 2 tbsp olive oil
- Juice of 1 lime
- Chimichurri
- ½ tsp salt
- ¼ cup olive oil
- 2 garlic cloves
- ¼ cup red onion, chopped
- ¼ cup red wine vinegar
- ½ tsp pepper
- 2 cups parsley
- ¼ tsp red pepper flakes

Directions:

1. Process the chimichurri ingredients in a blender until smooth; set aside. Combine shrimp, olive oil, and lime juice, in a bowl, and let marinate in the fridge for 30 minutes. Preheat your grill to medium. Add shrimp and cook about 2 minutes per side. Serve shrimp drizzled with the chimichurri sauce.

Nutrition Info:

- Info Per Servings 3.5g Carbs, 16g Protein, 20.3g Fat, 283 Calories

Cod With Balsamic Tomatoes

Servings: 4

Cooking Time: 30 Minutes

Ingredients:

- 4 center-cut bacon strips, chopped
- 4 cod fillets
- 2 cups grape tomatoes, halved
- 2 tablespoons balsamic vinegar
- 4 tablespoons olive oil
- 1/2 teaspoon salt
- 1/4 teaspoon pepper

Directions:

1. In a large skillet, heat olive oil and cook bacon over medium heat until crisp, stirring occasionally.
2. Remove with a slotted spoon; drain on paper towels.
3. Sprinkle fillets with salt and pepper. Add fillets to bacon drippings; cook over medium-high heat until fish just begins to flake easily with a fork, 4-6 minutes on each side. Remove and keep warm.
4. Add tomatoes to skillet; cook and stir until tomatoes are softened, 2-4 minutes. Stir in vinegar; reduce heat to medium-low. Cook until sauce is thickened, 1-2 minutes longer.
5. Serve cod with tomato mixture and bacon.

Nutrition Info:

- Info Per Servings 5g Carbs, 26g Protein, 30.4g Fat, 442 Calories

Baked Codfish With Lemon

Serves: 4

Cooking Time:25 Minutes

Ingredients:

- 4 fillets codfish
- 1 teaspoon salt
- 1 teaspoon pepper
- 2 tablespoons olive oil
- 2 teaspoons dried basil
- 2 tablespoons melted butter
- 1 teaspoon dried thyme
- 1/3 teaspoon onion powder
- 2 lemons, juiced
- lemon wedges, for garnish

Directions:

1. Preheat the oven to 400°F.
2. In a medium bowl combine the lemon juice, onion powder, olive oil, dried basil and thyme. Stir well. Season the fillets with salt and pepper.
3. Top each fillet into the mixture. Then place the fillets into a medium baking dish, greased with melted butter.
4. Bake the codfish fillets for 15-20 minutes. Serve with fresh lemon wedges. Enjoy!

Nutrition Info:

- Per serving: 3.9g Carbs; 21.2g Protein; 23.6g Fat; 308 Calories

Parmesan Fish Bake

Servings: 4

Cooking Time: 40 Minutes

Ingredients:

- Cooking spray
- 2 salmon fillets, cubed
- 3 white fish, cubed
- 1 broccoli, cut into florets
- 1 tbsp butter, melted
- Pink salt and black pepper to taste
- 1 cup crème fraiche
- ¼ cup grated Parmesan cheese
- Grated Parmesan cheese for topping

Directions:

1. Preheat oven to 400ºF and grease an 8 x 8 inches casserole dish with cooking spray. Toss the fish cubes and broccoli in butter and season with salt and pepper to taste. Spread in the greased dish.
2. Mix the crème fraiche with Parmesan cheese, pour and smear the cream on the fish, and sprinkle with some more Parmesan. Bake for 25 to 30 minutes until golden brown on top, take the dish out, sit for 5 minutes and spoon into plates. Serve with lemon-mustard asparagus.

Nutrition Info:

- Info Per Servings 4g Carbs, 28g Protein, 17g Fat, 354 Calories

Salmon Panzanella

Servings: 4

Cooking Time: 22 Minutes

Ingredients:

- 1 lb skinned salmon, cut into 4 steaks each
- 1 cucumber, peeled, seeded, cubed
- Salt and black pepper to taste
- 8 black olives, pitted and chopped
- 1 tbsp capers, rinsed
- 2 large tomatoes, diced
- 3 tbsp red wine vinegar
- ¼ cup thinly sliced red onion
- 3 tbsp olive oil
- 2 slices day-old zero carb bread, cubed
- ¼ cup thinly sliced basil leaves

Directions:

1. Preheat a grill to 350ºF and prepare the salad. In a bowl, mix the cucumbers, olives, pepper, capers, tomatoes, wine vinegar, onion, olive oil, bread, and basil leaves. Let sit for the flavors to incorporate.

2. Season the salmon steaks with salt and pepper; grill them on both sides for 8 minutes in total. Serve the salmon steaks warm on a bed of the veggies' salad.

Nutrition Info:

- Info Per Servings 3.1g Carbs, 28.5g Protein, 21.7g Fat, 338 Calories

Shrimp Stuffed Zucchini

Servings: 4

Cooking Time: 56 Minutes

Ingredients:

- 4 medium zucchinis
- 1 lb small shrimp, peeled, deveined
- 1 tbsp minced onion
- 2 tsp butter
- ¼ cup chopped tomatoes
- Salt and black pepper to taste
- 1 cup pork rinds, crushed
- 1 tbsp chopped basil leaves
- 2 tbsp melted butter

Directions:

1. Preheat the oven to 350ºF and trim off the top and bottom ends of the zucchinis. Lay them flat on a chopping board, and cut a ¼ -inch off the top to create a boat for the stuffing. Scoop out the seeds with a spoon and set the zucchinis aside.

2. Melt the firm butter in a small skillet and sauté the onion and tomato for 6 minutes. Transfer the mixture to a bowl and add the shrimp, half of the pork rinds, basil leaves, salt, and pepper.

3. Combine the ingredients and stuff the zucchini boats with the mixture. Sprinkle the top of the boats with the remaining pork rinds and drizzle the melted butter over them.

4. Place them on a baking sheet and bake them for 15 to 20 minutes. The shrimp should no longer be pink by this time. Remove the zucchinis after and serve with a tomato and mozzarella salad.

Nutrition Info:

- Info Per Servings 3.2g Carbs, 24.6g Protein, 14.4g Fat, 135 Calories

Sour Cream Salmon With Parmesan

Servings: 4

Cooking Time: 25 Minutes

Ingredients:

- 1 cup sour cream
- ½ tbsp minced dill
- ½ lemon, zested and juiced
- Pink salt and black pepper to season
- 4 salmon steaks
- ½ cup grated Parmesan cheese

Directions:

1. Preheat oven to 400ºF and line a baking sheet with parchment paper; set aside. In a bowl, mix the sour cream, dill, lemon zest, juice, salt and pepper, and set aside.

2. Season the fish with salt and black pepper, drizzle lemon juice on both sides of the fish and arrange them in the baking sheet. Spread the sour cream mixture on each fish and sprinkle with Parmesan.

3. Bake the fish for 15 minutes and after broil the top for 2 minutes with a close watch for a nice a brown color. Plate the fish and serve with buttery green beans.

Nutrition Info:

- Info Per Servings 1.2g Carbs, 16.2g Protein, 23.4g Fat, 288 Calories

Bacon And Salmon Bites

Serves: 2

Cooking Time: 15 Minutes

Ingredients:

- 1 salmon fillets
- 4 bacon slices, halved
- 2 tbsp chopped cilantro
- Seasoning:
- ¼ tsp salt
- 1/8 tsp ground black pepper

Directions:

1. Turn on the oven, then set it to 350 °F, and let it preheat.Meanwhile, cut salmon into bite-size pieces, then wrap each piece with a half slice of bacon, secure with a toothpick and season with salt and black pepper.Take a baking sheet, place prepared salmon pieces on it and bake for 13 to 15 minutes until nicely browned and thoroughly cooked.When done, sprinkle cilantro over salmon and serve.

Nutrition Info:

- 1 g Carbs; 10 g Protein; 9 g Fats; 120 Calories

Salmon And Cauliflower Rice Pilaf

Servings: 4

Cooking Time: 25 Minutes

Ingredients:

- 1 cauliflower head, shredded
- ¼ cup dried vegetable soup mix
- 1 cup chicken broth
- 1 pinch saffron
- 1-lb wild salmon fillets
- 6 tbsp olive oil
- Pepper and salt to taste

Directions:

1. Place a heavy-bottomed pot on medium-high fire and add all ingredients and mix well.
2. Bring to a boil, lower fire to a simmer, and simmer for 10 minutes.
3. Turn off fire, shred salmon, adjust seasoning to taste.
4. Let it rest for 5 minutes.
5. Fluff again, serve, and enjoy.

Nutrition Info:

- Info Per Servings 4.7g Carbs, 31.8g Protein, 31.5g Fat, 429 Calories

Steamed Asparagus And Shrimps

Servings: 6

Cooking Time: 15 Minutes

Ingredients:

- 1-pound shrimps, peeled and deveined
- 1 bunch asparagus, trimmed
- ½ tablespoon Cajun seasoning
- 2 tablespoons butter
- 5 tablespoons oil
- Salt and pepper to taste

Directions:

1. In a heat-proof dish that fits inside the saucepan, add all ingredients. Mix well.
2. Place a large saucepan on the medium-high fire. Place a trivet inside the saucepan and fill the pan halfway with water. Cover and bring to a boil.
3. Cover dish with foil and place on a trivet.
4. Cover pan and steam for 10 minutes. Let it rest in pan for another 5 minutes.
5. Serve and enjoy.

Nutrition Info:

- Info Per Servings 1.1g Carbs, 15.5g Protein, 15.8g Fat, 204.8 Calories

Desserts And Drinks Recipes

<u>Smarties Cookies</u>

Servings: 8

Cooking Time: 10 Mins

Ingredients:

- 1/4 cup. butter
- 1/2 cup. almond flour
- 1 tsp. vanilla essence
- 12 oz. bag of smarties
- 1 cup. stevia
- 1/4 tsp. baking powder

Directions:

1. Sift in flour and baking powder in a bowl, then stir through butter and mix until well combined.
2. Whisk in stevia and vanilla essence , stir until thick.
3. Then add the smarties and use your hand to mix and divide into small balls.
4. Bake until completely cooked, about 10 minutes. Let it cool and serve.

Nutrition Info:

- Info Per Servings 20.77g Carbs, 3.7g Protein, 11.89g Fat, 239 Calories

<u>Italian Greens And Yogurt Shake</u>

Servings: 1

Cooking Time: 0 Minutes

Ingredients:

- ½ cup half and half
- ½ cup Italian greens
- 1 packet Stevia, or more to taste
- 1 tbsp hemp seeds
- 3 tbsp coconut oil
- 1 cup water

Directions:

1. Add all ingredients in a blender.
2. Blend until smooth and creamy.
3. Serve and enjoy.

Nutrition Info:

- Info Per Servings 10.3g Carbs, 5.2g Protein, 46.9g Fat, 476 Calories

Lettuce Green Shake

Servings: 1
Cooking Time: 0 Minutes
Ingredients:

- ¾ cup whole milk yogurt
- 2 cups 5-lettuce mix salad greens
- 3 tbsp MCT oil
- 1 tbsp chia seeds
- 1 ½ cups water
- 1 packet Stevia, or more to taste

Directions:

1. Add all ingredients in a blender.
2. Blend until smooth and creamy.
3. Serve and enjoy.

Nutrition Info:

- Info Per Servings 6.1g Carbs, 8.1g Protein, 47g Fat, 483 Calories

Coconut Cheesecake

Servings: 12
Cooking Time: 4 Hours And 50 Minutes
Ingredients:

- Crust
- 2 egg whites
- ¼ cup erythritol
- 3 cups desiccated coconut
- 1 tsp coconut oil
- ¼ cup melted butter
- Filling:
- 3 tbsp lemon juice
- 6 ounces raspberries
- 2 cups erythritol
- 1 cup whipped cream
- Zest of 1 lemon
- 24 ounces cream cheese

Directions:

1. Apply the coconut oil to the bottom and sides of a springform pan. Line with parchment paper. Preheat your oven to 350°F and mix all crust ingredients. Pour the crust into the pan.
2. Bake for about 25 minutes; then let cool.
3. Meanwhile, beat the cream cheese with an electric mixer until soft. Add the lemon juice, zest, and erythritol.
4. Fold the whipped cream into the cheese cream mixture. Fold in the raspberries gently. Spoon the filling into the baked and cooled crust. Place in the fridge for 4 hours.

Nutrition Info:

- Info Per Servings 3g Carbs, 5g Protein, 25g Fat, 256 Calories

Vanilla Ice Cream

Servings: 4
Cooking Time: 50 Minutes + Cooling Time
Ingredients:

- ½ cup smooth peanut butter
- ½ cup swerve
- 3 cups half and half
- 1 tsp vanilla extract
- 2 pinches salt

Directions:

1. Beat peanut butter and swerve in a bowl with a hand mixer until smooth. Gradually whisk in half and half until thoroughly combined. Mix in vanilla and salt. Pour mixture into a loaf pan and freeze for 45 minutes until firmed up. Scoop into glasses when ready to eat and serve.

Nutrition Info:

- Info Per Servings 6g Carbs, 13g Protein, 23g Fat, 290 Calories

Strawberry-choco Shake

Servings: 1

Cooking Time: 0 Minutes

Ingredients:

- ½ cup heavy cream, liquid
- 1 tbsp cocoa powder
- 1 packet Stevia, or more to taste
- 4 strawberries, sliced
- 1 tbsp coconut flakes, unsweetened
- 1 ½ cups water
- 3 tbsps coconut oil

Directions:

1. Add all ingredients in a blender.
2. Blend until smooth and creamy.
3. Serve and enjoy.

Nutrition Info:

- Info Per Servings 10.1g Carbs, 2.6g Protein, 65.3g Fat, 610 Calories

Coconut-melon Yogurt Shake

Servings: 1

Cooking Time: 0 Minutes

Ingredients:

- ¼ cup half and half
- 3 tbsp coconut oil
- ½ cup melon, slices
- 1 tbsp coconut flakes, unsweetened
- 1 tbsp chia seeds
- 1 ½ cups water
- 1 packet Stevia, or more to taste

Directions:

1. Add all ingredients in a blender.
2. Blend until smooth and creamy.
3. Serve and enjoy.

Nutrition Info:

- Info Per Servings 8g Carbs, 2.4g Protein, 43g Fat, 440 Calories

Strawberry-coconut Shake

Servings: 1

Cooking Time: 0 Minutes

Ingredients:

- ½ cup whole milk yogurt
- 3 tbsp MCT oil
- ¼ cup strawberries, chopped
- 1 tbsp coconut flakes, unsweetened
- 1 tbsp hemp seeds
- 1 ½ cups water
- 1 packet Stevia, or more to taste

Directions:

1. Add all ingredients in a blender.
2. Blend until smooth and creamy.
3. Serve and enjoy.

Nutrition Info:

- Info Per Servings 10.2g Carbs, 6.4g Protein, 50.9g Fat, 511 Calories

Choco-coco Bars

Servings: 12
Cooking Time: 10 Minutes

Ingredients:

- 1/3 cup Virgin Coconut Oil, melted
- 2 cups shredded unsweetened coconut
- 2 droppers Liquid Stevia
- 2 droppers of Liquid Stevia
- 3 squares Baker's Unsweetened Chocolate
- 1 tablespoon oil

Directions:

1. Lightly grease an 8x8-inch silicone pan.
2. In a food processor, process shredded unsweetened coconut, coconut oil, and Stevia until it forms a dough. Transfer to prepared pan and press on the bottom to form a dough. Place in the freezer to set.
3. Meanwhile, in a microwave-safe Pyrex cup, place chocolate, coconut oil, and Stevia. Heat for 10-second intervals and mix well. Do not overheat, just until you have mixed the mixture thoroughly. Pour over dough.
4. Return to the freezer until set.
5. Serve and enjoy.

Nutrition Info:

- Info Per Servings 4.0g Carbs, 2.0g Protein, 22.0g Fat, 222 Calories

Eggless Strawberry Mousse

Servings: 6
Cooking Time: 6 Minutes + Cooling Time

Ingredients:

- 2 cups chilled heavy cream
- 2 cups fresh strawberries, hulled
- 5 tbsp erythritol
- 2 tbsp lemon juice
- ¼ tsp strawberry extract
- 2 tbsp sugar-free strawberry preserves

Directions:

1. Beat the heavy cream, in a bowl, with a hand mixer at high speed until a stiff peak forms, for about 1 minute; refrigerate immediately. Puree the strawberries in a blender and pour into a saucepan.
2. Add erythritol and lemon juice, and cook on low heat for 3 minutes while stirring continuously. Stir in the strawberry extract evenly, turn off heat and allow cooling. Fold in the whipped cream until evenly incorporated, and spoon into six ramekins. Refrigerate for 4 hours to solidify.
3. Garnish with strawberry preserves and serve immediately.

Nutrition Info:

- Info Per Servings 5g Carbs, 5g Protein, 24g Fat, 290 Calories

Strawberry And Basil Lemonade

Servings: 4
Cooking Time: 3 Minutes
Ingredients:

- 4 cups water
- 12 strawberries, leaves removed
- 1 cup fresh lemon juice
- ⅓ cup fresh basil
- ¾ cup swerve
- Crushed Ice
- Halved strawberries to garnish
- Basil leaves to garnish

Directions:

1. Spoon some ice into 4 serving glasses and set aside. In a pitcher, add the water, strawberries, lemon juice, basil, and swerve. Insert the blender and process the ingredients for 30 seconds.
2. The mixture should be pink and the basil finely chopped. Adjust the taste and add the ice in the glasses. Drop 2 strawberry halves and some basil in each glass and serve immediately.

Nutrition Info:

- Info Per Servings 5.8g Carbs, 0.7g Protein, 0.1g Fat, 66 Calories

Keto Lemon Custard

Servings: 8
Cooking Time: 50 Minutes
Ingredients:

- 1 Lemon
- 6 large eggs
- 2 tbsp lemon zest
- 1 cup Lakanto
- 2 cups heavy cream

Directions:

1. Preheat oven to 300oF.
2. Mix all ingredients.
3. Pour mixture into ramekins.
4. Put ramekins into a dish with boiling water.
5. Bake in the oven for 45-50 minutes.
6. Let cool then refrigerate for 2 hours.
7. Use lemon slices as garnish.

Nutrition Info:

- Info Per Servings 4.0g Carbs, 7.0g Protein, 21.0g Fat, 233 Calories

Coconut Macadamia Nut Bombs

Servings: 4

Cooking Time: 0 Mins

Ingredients:

- 2 packets stevia
- 5 tbsps unsweetened coconut powder
- 10 tbsps coconut oil
- 3 tbsps chopped macadamia nuts
- Salt to taste

Directions:

1. Heat the coconut oil in a pan over medium heat. Add coconut powder, stevia and salt, stirring to combined well; then remove from heat.
2. Spoon mixture into a lined mini muffin pan. Place in the freezer for a few hours.
3. Sprinkle nuts over the mixture before serving.

Nutrition Info:

- Info Per Servings 0.2g Carbs, 1.1g Protein, 15.2g Fat, 143 Calories

Blackcurrant Iced Tea

Servings: 4

Cooking Time: 8 Minutes

Ingredients:

- 6 unflavored tea bags
- 2 cups water
- ½ cup sugar-free blackcurrant extract
- Swerve to taste
- Ice cubes for serving
- Lemon slices to garnish, cut on the side

Directions:

1. Pour the ice cubes in a pitcher and place it in the fridge.
2. Bring the water to boil in a saucepan over medium heat for 3 minutes and turn the heat off. Stir in the sugar to dissolve and steep the tea bags in the water for 2 minutes.
3. Remove the bags after and let the tea cool down. Stir in the blackcurrant extract until well incorporated, remove the pitcher from the fridge, and pour the mixture over the ice cubes.
4. Let sit for 3 minutes to cool and after, pour the mixture into tall glasses. Add some more ice cubes, place the lemon slices on the rim of the glasses, and serve the tea cold.

Nutrition Info:

- Info Per Servings 5g Carbs, 0g Protein, 0g Fat, 22 Calories

Mint Chocolate Protein Shake

Servings: 4
Cooking Time: 4 Minutes
Ingredients:

- 3 cups flax milk, chilled
- 3 tsp unsweetened cocoa powder
- 1 avocado, pitted, peeled, sliced
- 1 cup coconut milk, chilled
- 3 mint leaves + extra to garnish
- 3 tbsp erythritol
- 1 tbsp low carb Protein powder
- Whipping cream for topping

Directions:

1. Combine the milk, cocoa powder, avocado, coconut milk, mint leaves, erythritol, and protein powder into a blender, and blend for 1 minute until smooth.
2. Pour into serving glasses, lightly add some whipping cream on top, and garnish with mint leaves.

Nutrition Info:

- Info Per Servings 4g Carbs, 15g Protein, 14.5g Fat, 191 Calories

Berry-choco Goodness Shake

Servings: 1
Cooking Time: 0 Minutes
Ingredients:

- ½ cup half and half
- ¼ cup raspberries
- ¼ cup blackberry
- ¼ cup strawberries, chopped
- 3 tbsps avocado oil
- 1 packet Stevia, or more to taste
- 1 tbsp cocoa powder
- 1 ½ cups water

Directions:

1. Add all ingredients in a blender.
2. Blend until smooth and creamy.
3. Serve and enjoy.

Nutrition Info:

- Info Per Servings 7g Carbs, 4.4g Protein, 43.3g Fat, 450 Calories

Mixed Berry Nuts Mascarpone Bowl

Servings: 4

Cooking Time: 8 Minutes

Ingredients:

- 4 cups Greek yogurt
- liquid stevia to taste
- 1 ½ cups mascarpone cheese
- 1 ½ cups blueberries and raspberries
- 1 cup toasted pecans

Directions:

1. Mix the yogurt, stevia, and mascarpone in a bowl until evenly combined. Divide the mixture into 4 bowls, share the berries and pecans on top of the cream. Serve the dessert immediately.

Nutrition Info:

- Info Per Servings 5g Carbs, 20g Protein, 40g Fat, 480 Calories

Lemony-avocado Cilantro Shake

Servings: 1

Cooking Time: 0 Minutes

Ingredients:

- ½ cup half and half
- 1 packet Stevia, or more to taste
- ¼ avocado, meat scooped
- 1 tbsp chopped cilantro
- 3 tbsps coconut oil
- 1 ½ cups water

Directions:

1. Add all ingredients in a blender.
2. Blend until smooth and creamy.
3. Serve and enjoy.

Nutrition Info:

- Info Per Servings 8.4g Carbs, 4.4g Protein, 49g Fat, 501 Calories

Garden Greens & Yogurt Shake

Servings: 1

Cooking Time: 0 Minutes

Ingredients:

- 1 cup whole milk yogurt
- 1 cup Garden greens
- 3 tbsp MCT oil
- 1 tbsp flaxseed, ground
- 1 cup water
- 1 packet Stevia, or more to taste

Directions:

1. Add all ingredients in a blender.
2. Blend until smooth and creamy.
3. Serve and enjoy.

Nutrition Info:

- Info Per Servings 7.2g Carbs, 11.7g Protein, 53g Fat, 581 Calories

Blackberry Cheese Vanilla Blocks

Servings: 5
Cooking Time: 20mins
Ingredients:

- ½ cup blackberries
- 6 eggs
- 4 oz mascarpone cheese
- 1 tsp vanilla extract
- 4 tbsp stevia
- 8 oz melted coconut oil
- ½ tsp baking powder

Directions:

1. Except for blackberries, blend all ingredients in a blender until smooth.
2. Combine blackberries with blended mixture and transfer to a baking dish.
3. Bake blackberries mixture in the oven at 320°F for 20 minutes. Serve.

Nutrition Info:

- Info Per Servings 15g Carbs, 13g Protein, 4g Fat, 199 Calories

Almond Butter Fat Bombs

Servings: 4
Cooking Time: 3 Minutes + Cooling Time
Ingredients:

- ½ cup almond butter
- ½ cup coconut oil
- 4 tbsp unsweetened cocoa powder
- ½ cup erythritol

Directions:

1. Melt butter and coconut oil in the microwave for 45 seconds, stirring twice until properly melted and mixed. Mix in cocoa powder and erythritol until completely combined.
2. Pour into muffin moulds and refrigerate for 3 hours to harden.

Nutrition Info:

- Info Per Servings 2g Carbs, 4g Protein, 18.3g Fat, 193 Calories

Passion Fruit Cheesecake Slices

Servings: 8

Cooking Time: 2 Hours 30 Minutes

Ingredients:

- 1 cup crushed almond biscuits
- ½ cup melted butter
- Filling:
- 1 ½ cups cream cheese
- ¾ cup swerve
- 1 ½ whipping cream
- 1 tsp vanilla bean paste
- 4-6 tbsp cold water
- 1 tbsp gelatin powder
- Passionfruit Jelly
- 1 cup passion fruit pulp
- ¼ cup swerve confectioner's sugar
- 1 tsp gelatin powder
- ¼ cup water, room temperature

Directions:

1. Mix the crushed biscuits and butter in a bowl, spoon into a spring-form pan, and use the back of the spoon to level at the bottom. Set aside in the fridge. Put the cream cheese, swerve, and vanilla paste into a bowl, and use the hand mixer to whisk until smooth; set aside.

2. In a bowl, add 2 tbsp of cold water and sprinkle 1 tbsp of gelatin powder. Let dissolve for 5 minutes. Pour the gelatin liquid along with the whipping cream in the cheese mixture and fold gently.

3. Remove the spring-form pan from the refrigerator and pour over the mixture. Return to the fridge.

4. Repeat the dissolving process for the remaining gelatin and once your out of ingredients, pour the confectioner's sugar, and ¼ cup of water into it. Mix and stir in the passion fruit pulp.

5. Remove the cake again and pour the jelly over it. Swirl the pan to make the jelly level up. Place the pan back into the fridge to cool for 2 hours. When completely set, remove and unlock the spring-pan. Lift the pan from the cake and slice the dessert.

Nutrition Info:

- Info Per Servings 6.1g Carbs, 4.4g Protein, 18g Fat, 287 Calories

28-Day Meal Plan

Day 1
Breakfast: Middle Eastern Style Tuna Salad
Lunch: Red Wine Chicken
Dinner: Butternut Squash And Cauliflower Stew

Day 2
Breakfast: Zucchini Gratin With Feta Cheese
Lunch: Grilled Paprika Chicken With Steamed Broccoli
Dinner: Lemon Grilled Veggie

Day 3
Breakfast: Crunchy Pork Rind And Zucchini Sticks
Lunch: Habanero Chicken Wings
Dinner: Crispy-topped Baked Vegetables

Day 4
Breakfast: Cheesy Cauliflower Fritters
Lunch: Duck & Vegetable Casserole
Dinner: Vegetable Tempura

Day 5
Breakfast: Parmesan Crackers With Guacamole
Lunch: Garlic & Ginger Chicken With Peanut Sauce
Dinner: Coconut Cauliflower & Parsnip Soup

Day 6
Breakfast: Turkey Pastrami & Mascarpone Cheese Pinwheels
Lunch: One Pot Chicken With Mushrooms
Dinner: Creamy Almond And Turnip Soup

Day 7
Breakfast: Keto Caprese Salad
Lunch: Marinara Chicken Sausage
Dinner: Garlic And Greens

Day 8
Breakfast: Buttered Broccoli
Lunch: Pacific Chicken
Dinner: Coconut Chicken Soup

Day 9
Breakfast: Keto "cornbread"
Lunch: Avocado Cheese Pepper Chicken
Dinner: Caesar Salad With Smoked Salmon And Poached Eggs

Day 10
Breakfast: Basil Keto Crackers
Lunch: Chicken In White Wine Sauce
Dinner: Spinach Fruit Salad With Seeds

Day 11
Breakfast: Roasted String Beans, Mushrooms & Tomato Plate
Lunch: Chicken Cauliflower Bake
Dinner: Traditional Greek Salad

Day 12
Breakfast: Asian Glazed Meatballs
Lunch: Chicken In Creamy Spinach Sauce
Dinner: Watermelon And Cucumber Salad

Day 13
Breakfast: Baba Ganoush Eggplant Dip
Lunch: Chicken Cacciatore
Dinner: Pesto Arugula Salad

Day 14
Breakfast: Cajun Spiced Pecans
Lunch: Chicken Drumsticks In Tomato Sauce
Dinner: Fruit Salad With Poppy Seeds

Day 15

Breakfast: Cheesy Green Bean Crisps
Lunch: Rosemary Grilled Chicken
Dinner: Corn And Bacon Chowder

Day 16

Breakfast: Bacon Jalapeno Poppers
Lunch: Chicken With Green Sauce
Dinner: Celery Salad

Day 17

Breakfast: Parsnip And Carrot Fries With Aioli
Lunch: Chicken And Mushrooms
Dinner: Lobster Salad With Mayo Dressing

Day 18

Breakfast: Sriracha Tofu With Yogurt Sauce
Lunch: Chicken Garam Masala
Dinner: Balsamic Cucumber Salad

Day 19

Breakfast: Vegetable Greek Mousaka
Lunch: Lemon Threaded Chicken Skewers
Dinner: Beef Reuben Soup

Day 20

Breakfast: Cream Of Zucchini And Avocado
Lunch: Chili Lime Chicken
Dinner: Clam Chowder

Day 21

Breakfast: Walnut Tofu Sauté
Lunch: Roasted Chicken With Herbs
Dinner: Mushroom-broccoli Soup

Day 22

Breakfast: Stuffed Cremini Mushrooms
Lunch: Garlic Pork Chops With Mint Pesto
Dinner: Bacon And Pea Salad

Day 23

Breakfast: Kale Cheese Waffles
Lunch: Mushroom Beef Stew
Dinner: Green Mackerel Salad

Day 24

Breakfast: Avocado And Tomato Burritos
Lunch: Baked Pork Meatballs In Pasta Sauce
Dinner: Chicken And Cauliflower Rice Soup

Day 25

Breakfast: Vegetable Burritos
Lunch: White Wine Lamb Chops
Dinner: Garlic Chicken Salad

Day 26

Breakfast: Vegetarian Burgers
Lunch: Jamaican Pork Oven Roast
Dinner: Homemade Cold Gazpacho Soup

Day 27

Breakfast: Keto Pizza Margherita
Lunch: Garlicky Pork With Bell Peppers
Dinner: Chicken Stock And Green Bean Soup

Day 28

Breakfast: Keto Beefy Burritos
Lunch: Spicy Pork Stew With Spinach
Dinner: Sour Cream And Cucumbers

INDEX

D

E

F

G

Garden Greens & Yogurt Shake 86
Garlic & Ginger Chicken With Peanut Sauce 33
Garlic Aioli 66
Garlic And Greens 30
Garlic Chicken Salad 59
Garlic Pork Chops With Mint Pesto 42
Garlicky Pork With Bell Peppers 45
Greek Yogurt Dressing 62
Green Goddess Dressing 65
Green Jalapeno Sauce 64
Green Mackerel Salad 58
Grilled Flank Steak With Lime Vinaigrette 46
Grilled Paprika Chicken With Steamed Broccoli 31
Grilled Shrimp With Chimichurri Sauce 74
Grilled Spicy Eggplant 24
Guacamole 28

H

Habanero Chicken Wings 32
Herby Beef & Veggie Stew 49
Homemade Cold Gazpacho Soup 59

I

Italian Greens And Yogurt Shake 79

J

Jamaican Pork Oven Roast 44

K

Kale Cheese Waffles 27
Keto "cornbread" 15
Keto Beefy Burritos 44
Keto Caprese Salad 14
Keto Lemon Custard 83
Keto Pizza Margherita 30
Keto Ranch Dip 63
Keto Thousand Island Dressing 66
Ketogenic-friendly Gravy 67

L

Lemon Garlic Shrimp 73
Lemon Grilled Veggie 22
Lemon Tahini Sauce 68
Lemon Threaded Chicken Skewers 40

Lemony-avocado Cilantro Shake 86
Lettuce Green Shake 80
Lobster Salad With Mayo Dressing 55

M

Marinara Chicken Sausage 34
Middle Eastern Style Tuna Salad 12
Mint Chocolate Protein Shake 85
Mixed Berry Nuts Mascarpone Bowl 86
Mixed Roast Vegetables 17
Moroccan Beef Stew 47
Mushroom Beef Stew 42
Mushroom-broccoli Soup 56
Mustard-lemon Beef 49

O

One Pot Chicken With Mushrooms 33

P

Pacific Chicken 34
Parmesan Crackers With Guacamole 14
Parmesan Fish Bake 75
Parsnip And Carrot Fries With Aioli 20
Passion Fruit Cheesecake Slices 88
Peanut Sauce 65
Pesto Arugula Salad 54
Pizzaiola Steak Stew 50
Pork Chops And Peppers 47

R

Red Cabbage Tilapia Taco Bowl 70
Red Curry Halibut 70
Red Wine Chicken 31
Roasted Chicken With Herbs 41
Roasted Garlic Lemon Dip 63
Roasted String Beans, Mushrooms & Tomato Plate 16
Rosemary Grilled Chicken 38

S

Salmon And Cauliflower Rice Pilaf 78
Salmon Panzanella 76
Shrimp In Curry Sauce 71
Shrimp Stuffed Zucchini 76
Smarties Cookies 79
Sour Cream And Cucumbers 60
Sour Cream Salmon With Parmesan 77

Spicy Pork Stew With Spinach 45
Spicy Sea Bass With Hazelnuts 72
Spinach Fruit Salad With Seeds 52
Sriracha Mayo 61
Sriracha Tofu With Yogurt Sauce 22
Steamed Asparagus And Shrimps 78
Strawberry And Basil Lemonade 83
Strawberry-choco Shake 81
Strawberry-coconut Shake 81
Stuffed Cremini Mushrooms 26
Stuffed Jalapeno 21

T

Tasty Cauliflower Dip 29
Thyme-sesame Crusted Halibut 72
Tilapia With Olives & Tomato Sauce 70
Tomato Stuffed Avocado 28
Traditional Greek Salad 53
Tuna Salad With Lettuce & Olives 60
Turkey Pastrami & Mascarpone Cheese Pinwheels 14
Tzatziki 64

V

Vanilla Ice Cream 80
Vegetable Burritos 27
Vegetable Greek Mousaka 23
Vegetable Tempura 25
Vegetarian Burgers 28
Vegetarian Fish Sauce 68

W

Walnut Tofu Sauté 24
Watermelon And Cucumber Salad 53
White Wine Lamb Chops 43

Z

Zucchini Gratin With Feta Cheese 12

Printed in Great Britain
by Amazon

26301355R00053